Freud or Jung?

FREUD OR JUNG?

Edward Glover

Meridian Books

THE WORLD PUBLISHING COMPANY

CLEVELAND AND NEW YORK

A MERIDIAN BOOK

Published by The World Publishing Company
2231 West 110th Street, Cleveland, Ohio 44102
First Meridian printing September 1956
Eighth printing November 1965
Reprinted by arrangement with W. W. Norton & Company, Inc.
Library of Congress Catalog Card Number: 56-10017
Printed in the United States of America.   8FD1165

CONTENTS

CONTENTS

PREFACE

About eight years ago Cyril Connolly invited me to contribute to *Horizon* a critique of the psychology of Jung. 'I feel,' he wrote, 'that Jung's reputation has grown out of all proportion in the last few years because of that aspect of his work which is really a distortion of Freud's ideas by the injection into them of unscientific mystical feelings which make them popular, but which are antagonistic to the whole Freudian conception of psychology as a Science. It seems to me,' he continued, 'that only a really profound Freudian can unravel in the work of Jung those elements in which Jung's own desire for a religious, rather than a scientific, conception exists. I am also alarmed,' added Mr. Connolly, 'at the popularity of Jung's ideas in the Catholic Church, and among my literary friends who confuse the inspirational value of much of Jung's thought with the basic accuracy required of such thinking.'

I must confess that Mr. Connolly's project appealed to me for reasons of my own. Some twenty-five years earlier, when I was first responsible for organising the training of psycho-analytical students, I had suggested that every candidate should be instructed in the systems propounded by the then most important psycho-analytical schismatics, Jung, Adler and Rank. When I put this suggestion to Ernest Jones, then President of the British Psycho-analytical Society, that unbending champion and teacher of Freudian psychology rejected it with the brief comment, 'Why waste their time?' But I have never abandoned the view that students of psycho-anaylsis should not only be familiar with systems that are in opposition to Freudian principles but be able to say exactly what is wrong with them. As for those self-appointed lay critics who venture to pass summary judgement on the respective merits of various schools of clinical psychology, it does not seem too much to ask that they should first familiarise themselves with the

7

principles at stake. I therefore accepted Mr. Connolly's invitation, realising that it would enable me to achieve in some part my earlier ambition, without wasting anyone's time but my own—for it mortgaged the leisure intervals of two years to re-read either in translation or in the original the voluminous works of C. G. Jung.

When the time came to summarise the results of this exploration, it became apparent that the issues could not be made clear without a parallel statement of Freud's general theory of mind. It was also obvious that even with the most drastic pruning the critique could not be compressed into the space of a short essay. And so, taking advantage of Mr. Connolly's editorial complaisance, I proceeded to send him instalments of a prodigious length, promising each time that the next would be the last. Three of these were published in *Horizon* (Nos. 106, 107 and 111) and are included in Chapters I, II, III, VIII and IX of this book. The sections on Mental Mechanisms, Character Types, Dreams, Neuroses, Individuation, and Art, appear now for the first time. Projected chapters dealing with Jung's views on education, philosophy and other aspects of his *Weltanschauung* were abandoned when in course of writing it became clear that this would merely involve a tedious repetition of arguments that had already been extended in earlier sections.

No apology is offered for the often technicality of the presentation. I have endeavoured to state the position as clearly as possible; but have expressly refrained from sacrificing accuracy to over-simplification. Most of the problems of unconscious psychology are of their nature difficult to grasp, and there is nothing to be gained by pretending that they can be solved on the run. In any case, those who take upon themselves to pass judgement on psychological theories should not expect to be relieved of the tedium of following a difficult argument. Nevertheless, I am left with the uneasy feeling that I have not satisfied the terms of Mr. Connolly's brief. For, in the first place, I have been unable to find that Jung has injected anything into

8

Freud's ideas; in the second, I have not detected in Jung's writings any desire for a religious conception; and, in the third, I cannot find in Jung's thought any inspirational value that is not at the same time illusory. But that is to anticipate.

EDWARD GLOVER

I am indebted to Miss W. M. Geddes for her assiduous and discriminating labour in the collection and collation of references.—E.G.

CHAPTER I

INTRODUCTORY

THE appearance in these times of an essay on the psychology of Jung written by a Freudian calls for some explanation. Jung was one of the more spectacular psycho-analytical
schismatics; and for some years after he abandoned his early
devotion to Freudian theories the public was entertained
with acrimonious discussions between representatives of the
two 'schools'. For reasons that will be considered later this
gladiatorial phase has now passed. Under ordinary circumstances there would be no excuse for further polemical dis-
plays save the desirability of assessing from time to time and
as dispassionately as may be the progress of psychological
science, in particular of clinical psychology. And since the
pace of psychological discovery is unhappily slow this need
could well be met by a decennial review.

There are however two special circumstances which make
an assessment of the relative significance of Freud and of
Jung desirable at this juncture. The first is purely extrinsic,
the second intrinsic. However careful psychologists may be
not to derive from their work, or to countenance, more than
the most sparing scientific *Weltanschauung*, they cannot
prevent more enthusiastic searchers after a philosophy of
life pursuing their favourite pastime. Still less can they prevent the exploitation of their psychological theories by self-
appointed and tendentious commentators. And so from time
to time our quarterlies publish essays in which, for example,
the influence on modern thought of Freudian psychology or
of Jungian psychology, and sometimes the relation of these
psychological systems to the Marxian dialectic, is set forth
with considerable dexterity if not always with accurate
understanding.

Much more excusable is the attempt of writers on aesthetics to supplement the rather scrappy formulations on these

11

subjects that are thinly scattered throughout the writings of Freud and, more plentifully, in those of Jung. These unsolicited efforts to apply and expand psychological theory are dictated to some extent by a not altogether unjustifiable impatience with the slowness of psychological discovery. Particularly in the field of aesthetics, Freudian formulations have been strictly limited to pointing out the infantile and unconscious origins of the sublimatory process and the part played by creative sublimations in preventing, controlling or assuaging unconscious conflict, in other words, in helping to maintain peace of mind. Beyond that the Freudian has not seen fit to go. Nor, to put it quite frankly, is the average analyst qualified to do so. Like most psychiatrists, he has neither the cultural feeling nor the type of education necessary to pursue these matters beyond the limits of his professional vision. The average psycho-analyst is a craftsman, not an artist.

Unfortunately such non-analytical writers as have the necessary cultural background seldom possess the technical qualifications which would justify their taking the law into their own hands. Thus in a recent article on the psychology of surrealism[1] the author mars an otherwise perfectly sensible essay by neglecting to distinguish between *unconscious conflict*, a universal phenomenon marking the opposition between man's instinctual inheritance and the limitations imposed on him by reality and, on the other hand, a *neurotic solution of excessive conflict* due to a combination of constitutional causes, developmental flaws in the mental apparatus and a precipitating factor of frustration. 'It is time,' he says, 'to point out and underline the gross limitations of Freudianism in its approach to art. Its study of the pathological led to the formulation of an aesthetic that looked upon the artist as a neurotic and art as a case of sublimation.' Inevitably the author draws comparison with Jung: 'Since Jung rejects the Freudian conception of the unconscious, he also objects to the theory that art is an

[1] Glicksberg. *Polemic*, No. 8.

attempt to find a surrogate for an unsatisfactory reality.'
And again 'It is his (Jung's) belief, *and here he is eminently
sound*, that a work of art exists in its own right'. The casual
reader is thus left with the impression that Freudian values
have been perverted by an excessive concern with disordered products, a hackneyed criticism this, and that by
contrast Jungian values are in some way or other 'healthier',
or, at any rate, more suitable to the understanding of
aesthetics.

An even more regrettable, and from the creative point of
view disastrous, consequence of ill-digested psychological
information is manifested in the productions of writers and
artists who have been either profoundly intrigued by
psychological interpretations of the central themes of human
conflict, or fascinated by the products of associative thinking
both visual and verbal. The most striking examples are provided by surrealist writers and painters who are apparently
under the impression that by adopting the technique of
'free presentation' they can either directly express unconscious content or quicken the creative process. As the very
self-consciousness of many surrealist presentations goes to
show, this misapprehension is based on an incapacity to
distinguish clearly between the *primary processes* that
govern unconscious function and the *secondary processes*
that regulate the activity of the (pre)conscious mind.[1]
Once the secondary processes are established, they cannot be

[1] In the primary process the energy activating unconscious content
constantly strives for discharge and in so doing makes use of certain
primitive mechanisms, in particular 'condensation' and 'displacement'.
In the unconscious system no considerations of time, reality or logic
exist: no contradictions are recognized: unconscious systems are governed solely by the pleasure-principle and the repetition compulsion. In
the secondary processes characteristic of the pre-conscious system the
ego blocks the tendency to discharge and develops faculties of logical
and intelligent judgement. These processes are accelerated by the
development of the reality principle which is derived from continued
experience of frustration, and by the organization of the power of
speech. The combined operation of primary and secondary processes is
best observed in dream-life.

completely abrogated even in the most profound mental regressions. The most distorted products of schizophrenic imagination include elaborate contributions from the pre-conscious system of the mind. On this matter of 'giving direct expression to the unconscious', it can only be said that where the schizophrenic fails it is not likely the artist will succeed.

Still greater confusion of thought is displayed by those writers who have been seduced by the attractions of the case-history. Forgetting that a case-history is a means to a professional rather than an æsthetic end, i.e., a functional balance-sheet to be read in terms of effective adaptation, they prostitute whatever artistic talent or dramatic sense they may possess to a professional under-lining of clinical themes. A recent reviewer of the prose works of Pierre Jean Jouve remarks: 'No doubt it is a function of the novelist to incorporate the new discoveries of depth psychology in his work, but he can do this only by transmuting it, by seizing that essence of artistic truth which lies entangled among the jargon.' Actually it is no part of the function of the novelist to do so; rather it should be his concern to express the artistic truth which lies entangled in his own mind. Other-wise more likely than not he will entangle the mind of his reader in psychological confusions. Jouve himself, it would seem, is passionately devoted to the theories of Freud and combines this devotion not only with a highly individualized form of Christian ethic but with an archaic conception of atonement which, as we shall see, is reminiscent of the archetypical metaphysics of Jung.

Here then is a partial justification for shaking the old bones of the Freud-Jung controversy. Obviously under a free press there can be no interference with the liberty of the subject to produce essays in applied psycho-analysis or in applied Jungian psychology or both; but at least the subject should possess an accurate knowledge of the principles he is applying, and understand to what extent the differences between the two schools are irreconcilable.

14

The second circumstance justifying a reassessment of the contributions to psychology of Freud and of Jung is, as has been suggested, essentially intrinsic in nature, that is to say, it is a factor inherent in the evolution of psychological science. It is, by the same token, a typical post-war reaction, a manifestation of that expiatory process which comes on the heels of major catastrophes whether these be natural or man-made. Experience of two world wars has demonstrated that after the cessation of hostilities social activities are governed by two opposing tendencies: to continue war-making in an unofficial and less destructive form and to engage somewhat aggressively in making peace. On the one hand, the sudden diversion of hostility from the common enemy leads to every variety of social upheaval; on the other, surplus drives towards peace-making, being denied effective diplomatic expression, are diverted to any field of endeavour where conflict of one kind or another prevails. Not the least intriguing form of surplus peace-making is to be observed in the field of psychological science. Certainly it cannot be denied that pre-war psychology was distinguished by a smouldering warfare and that there is nowadays a signifi-cant drive towards composition of psychological differences. After the United Nations a United Psychology.

Before we lightly accept the assumption that this new development is motivated solely by scientific ideals, it is well to review the origin of those conflicts which, up to the commencement of the Second World War, embittered the relations of psychological schools. For certainly no new psychological discoveries were made in wartime that would justify the composition of scientific differences. On the con-trary and despite the wartime craze for psychiatry, the war period was completely barren of psychological progress. Psychology in fact embarked on one of those headlong re-gressions that are inevitable when military necessity rather than scientific ideals provides the mainspring for psycho-logical action. The only conclusion to be drawn from the technique of wartime psychiatry is that necessity is the mother of compromise, a conclusion sufficiently axiomatic to be in no particular need of corroboration.

But if no new discoveries have been made to justify a collaborationist movement within a conflict-ridden science, we are faced with the alternative assumptions either that earlier conflicts were non-essential or that for one reason or another they are now in process of being glossed over. *In my opinion these earlier conflicts were inevitable and fundamental.* Despite the passage of time the resistance to Freud's discovery of the unconscious mind remains unabated both within and without the psycho-analytic movement. Within, it is signalized by schisms and controversies; outside, Freud's theories are either openly opposed, or discreetly watered down or again mingled with non-analytical contributions to form a compost of contradictory assumptions.

It is to this last form of opposition that the 'eclectic' psychologist has devoted his reactionary energies. Preening himself on his scientific detachment and his capacity to take only the 'best' from each school, the eclectic is not very much concerned whether a little bit of Freud and a little bit of Jung when dovetailed with little bits of Adler or Stekel forms a crazy pavement so long as the pavement offers a short cut to therapeutic success, a criterion which, as we shall see, does not establish the validity of any theory. The eclectic in fact does more than any other practitioner to obstruct the progress of clinical psychology. It is no service to psychology to gloss over fundamental differences. On the contrary it only obscures a fundamental fact, namely, that *so long as objective psychologies of the unconscious exist there are bound to be irreconcilable differences between those who support them unreservedly, those who merely render them lip-service and those who repudiate them.*

Now although it is too soon to observe the influence on the lay public of professional efforts to consolidate psychological theory, it is safe to assume that the attitude of the average reader will be receptive to the new eclecticism. And this means in effect that with the passage of time, the

16

INTRODUCTORY

most comforting theories of mental function will tend to resume their earlier sway. This tendency will no doubt be sedulously fostered by the Churches. Freud's discovery of the unconscious mind had confronted theologians with some awkward problems and already there is some evidence that Roman Catholic priests when called on by their parishioners to deliver judgement on the psychologies of Jung and Freud, being unable summarily to reject both systems, throw their weight on the side of Jungian theory which in some way or another is felt to be closer to religious belief than the 'deterministic' psychology of Freud. Admittedly it is difficult to assess public opinion in these matters with accuracy; but in the absence of more exact information it is perhaps legitimate to quote from the public utterances of an apostle of the mid-brows. Broadcasting recently on the subject of Jung, Mr. J. B. Priestley delivered himself of the following opinions: ' . . . he (Jung) seems to me not only one of the great original thinkers of our time but also one of its few liberators', ' . . . he has brought the West closer to the immemorial and profoundly intuitive East; and has discovered at least one way out of the nightmare maze in which modern Western man was beginning to lose himself.'

Speaking of Jung's concept of the Collective Unconscious, Priestley remarks, 'I for one find a liberating force in this theory . . . It enlarges man instead of cutting him down . . . It (the collective unconscious) is an essential part of our real selves . . . This is what all the great religions have told us and here Jung, pursuing a piece of scientific research to its logical conclusions, has come close to religion.' And again: 'perhaps Jung's greatest achievement is this—that using the instrument of modern Western man, the scientific intellect, he has cleared a way through dark jungles into blue mountain air, where below, on the spiral mountain path of man's inquiries into the spirit . . .' And so on in the Jungian idiom. As might be expected from all this, Priestley dismisses Freud with a few summary remarks unequalled for their compact ignorance. Thus '(Jung's) unconscious . . . was

17

clearly not the unconscious that the Freudians described, a mere small lumber-room for the conscious mind'. '(Freud's) theory . . . was far too limited.' And the like.

Now it is vain to expect apostles to display a sense of scientific responsibility. Their primary allegiance is to their creed. Having read and re-read Jung 'with increasing pleasure and profit' Mr. Priestley naturally wishes to share with his listeners the comfort he, as a 'battered and baffled fellow-man, has extracted from his reading. Indeed he goes out of his way to disclaim authority, and with authority, of course, responsibility. His address begins in fact with a short sentence that might have come more appropriately at its end. 'I am not a psychologist,' he says. True enough; but his millions of listeners equally battered and baffled are likely to take this modest disclaimer as an additional proof of common sense. Unable, as Mr. Priestley is unable, to distinguish which parts of Jungian psychology are derived from Freud and which parts are peculiar to Jung, they are likely to fall back on and fortify earlier prejudices, to regard Jung as a great mystic who is also a great liberator and Freud as the purveyor of a diseased psychology, dull, dry, disappointing and probably dirty.

CRITERIA OF ASSESSMENT

Should the foregoing considerations persuade the reader that the time is ripe to reopen the Freud-Jung controversy, he may well demand to be provided with some criteria with which to carry out his assessments. How, in fact, does one set about comparing one psychological theory or system with another?

The first step in this direction is to rid oneself of a natural prejudice. The psychologies of Freud and Jung having been derived originally from study of disordered mental states it was at first natural to think that the validity of a clinical theory could be determined by the results of treatment based on that theory. But alas! the therapeutic criterion was to prove a broken reed. The most satisfying theory of schizo-phrenia, for example, does not overcome the average schizo-phrenic's inaccessibility to analytical influence. The 'gain from illness' unconsciously extracted from an apparently simple psychoneurosis may render the latter refractory to treatment by any method. For the matter of that, a visit to Brighton or an intercurrent attack of influenza may coincide with a remission in an apparently chronic mental disorder; yet he would be a hardy speculator who would make such observations the basis of a theory of psychological climatology or of psycho-toxic function, hardier still to make them the basis of a general theory of mental activity.

The truth is that no psychological theory is worth the paper it is written on unless it can give an objective account of the structure, function and dynamics of mind, can trace the stages of mental development from infancy to senescence, can indi-cate the main factors giving rise to mental disorder and correlate these with the mechanisms responsible for the more significant manifestations of normal mental life both indivi-dual and social.

At this point a difficulty arises which might appear to wreck any attempt to apply these criteria in a comparative study of psychological theories. The 'normal' psychologist, for example, whose most daring excursions into the terri-tories of mind have never taken him beyond the superficial layers of the pre-conscious where much that he finds is familiar, logical and safe, might, indeed I think does, claim that his descriptive systems satisfy most of these standards. Yet as Freud once remarked, 'A psychology which cannot explain dreams is also useless for the elucidation of normal psychical activity and has no claim to be called a science'.[1] In fact since Freud's discovery of the unconscious mind, no account of mental function can be regarded as satisfactory which does not include a full description of unconscious processes. To the Jungian partisan such an axiom might

[1] *The Question of Lay-Analysis*. (Translation.) Imago Publishing Co. 1947.

appear to prejudice the issue by insisting on the validity of Freud's conception of the unconscious: yet in fact it does not prevent the institution of comparisons between Freudian and Jungian systems. It is not disputed that prior to his break with Freud, Jung freely accepted Freudian views. That Jung's subsequent formulations deviated in fundamental respects from his earlier views, so far from being an obstacle to comparative study, provides us with a convenient starting point for comparison. Indeed sooner or later we are bound to ask two questions, first, whether the concept of the unconscious advanced by Jung after his deviation from Freud bears any resemblance to the Freudian concept of the unconscious, and second, whether these parts of Jungian theory theory which bear no resemblance to or even contradict Freudian theory constitute, as is popularly assumed, an improvement on Freudian concepts.

CHAPTER II

MENTAL STRUCTURE

As has already been indicated, the description of mental processes involves a threefold approach to the subject. Although the psychologist is not concerned with the locality of mind, he finds himself compelled to postulate for purposes of presentation a certain degree of mental organization which can be conveniently referred to as mental *structure.* Having done so he is then compelled to describe the *energies* which activate this organization or apparatus. Once embarked on this process he cannot stop short of describing the *mechanisms* by which the mental apparatus regulates these energies. This threefold approach constitutes what Freud termed the *metapsychological* approach to the descriptive data, either reported or introspected, that constitute the raw material of psychology.[1]

To begin then with the *structure of mind*, it may be noted that this concept was an inevitable consequence of Freud's discovery of unconscious 'content'. For if it can be demonstrated that ideas and potential affects exist apart from consciousness, yet can be made conscious by the use of a technique which overcomes certain 'resistances', it is legitimate to postulate an *unconscious system* of the mind (*ucs*). This Freud did, adding that the resistances indicated the existence of a barrier of repression, a kind of psychic frontier. Henceforward *consciousness* was regarded as another system of mind having psychic perceptual functions to perform

[1] The account of Freudian principles given in this essay is drawn from the writings of Freud and from those of his followers who have applied those principles without deviation. It specifically excludes some recent theories of child psychology which have gained currency amongst a small group of psycho-analysts in this country. In the writer's view this Kleinian system constitutes a deviation from Freudian principles and practice, combining, it is interesting to note, some of the errors of both Rank and Jung.

(*pcpt-cs*). Between these two systems lay yet another, the content of which though at any given moment descriptively unconscious yet could be recalled more or less at will. This he called the *pre-conscious system* (*pcs*), avoiding thereby the term 'sub-conscious' which confuses the vital distinction between the conscious and the true (dynamic) unconscious. This tripartite division constituted Freud's first rough outline of the *mental apparatus*, an organization whose function it is to receive the incoming charges of (internal) instinct and stimulations coming from the external world, to master these charges and stimulations and to procure them satisfactory discharge (adaptation).

At this stage the position of the ego was not very clearly defined. It was regarded as a surface organ of the psyche, including the whole territory of the pre-conscious system, having instincts and mechanisms of its own which were set in action not only by the external necessities of life but by any irruption of unconscious or repressed instincts from the unconscious system (*ucs*) that threatened the ego with danger. Further investigations however convinced Freud that the unconscious was not comprised solely of primitive instincts and repressed derivatives and that a large part of the ego itself, including that part responsible for repression, was itself unconscious in both the descriptive and the dynamic senses of the term. It was at this time that Freud published his description of the *super-ego*, an unconscious institution that performs the function of scrutinizing instinctual urges and, according to its standards, instigates the unconscious ego to acts of defence calculated to prevent the break through into the (pre)conscious system of primitive instinctual derivatives. Without abandoning the concept of a mental apparatus or in any way discounting the importance of repression, Freud decided to abandon the concept of specifically ego-instincts, and to include all instinctual forces within a special mental system which he termed the *Id*. (the It). The term was adopted to indicate the impersonal (non-ego) nature of the system. However deeply the Ego might penetrate the Id, however unconscious parts of the ego might be, it was still a surface organ, a psychic cortex to the Id, a special agency of the psyche turned directly towards the external world, in a word, a psychic organ of adaptation.

This new tripartite division (Id, Super-ego and Ego) represented an immeasurable advance. Thenceforward the energies of Freud and of his followers were concentrated on tracing stage by stage the early development of *ego-institutions*, for already the nature of Id instincts had been roughly outlined, in particular the early forms and modifications of infantile sexual instinct and the hates and rivalries that are engendered by these libidinal instincts. It was now possible to institute a parallel series of investigations, correlating stages in development of infantile impulse with stages in the development of the ego and super-ego, indicating *en route* the particular unconscious mechanisms characteristic of mental defence at each stage. Here was indeed a focal point starting from which the student might, according to his predilection, trace the history of character and conscience, or discover etiological formulae that would account for disorders varying in depth from schizophrenia to inferiority feeling, from homicidal psychopathy to social disagreeableness, from infantile perversion to 'platonic love'. In a word it became possible to abandon old and misleading classifications of mental phenomena based on mainly descriptive criteria and to substitute for these metapsychological classifications that will some day become Linnaean in magnitude and complexity.

Here then in brief outline is an account of what Priestley, pontificating on Jung, steps aside to describe as a 'limited' theory based on an unconscious system that is a mere 'lumber-room' to the conscious. Let us see how the Freudian lumber-room compares with the Jungian edifice which, according to Priestley, contains 'treasures of the utmost value' to his 'battered and baffled fellow-men'.

Approaching his concepts in order of descending magnitude,[1] we find that the focal point or perhaps one should say the final psychological product of Jung's entire system is the *Self* or Subject. This comprises both personal and racial elements and includes the entire psyche both conscious and unconscious. The *psyche* in its turn is the totality of all psychological processes and, since all experience is psychic, includes all experience. It is broader than and contains the *soul*, which in turn is the personality-attitude displayed by the individual to his unconscious. *Mind* is equated with conscious psychological activity, consciousness or intelligence. The psyche is then subdivided into three *systems*; the *Conscious*, the *Personal Unconscious* and the racial or *Collective Unconscious*. Scrutinizing these systems to determine the position of the Ego, we find that the outermost side of the conscious system is made up of a function-complex called the *Persona*. It is exclusively concerned with the individual's relation to the object world but is by no means identical with the individual. Here at last we find the Ego. The ego is surrounded by the mantle of the persona, a focal point for the conscious system;[2] yet it is the unitary totality of our personal psychosomatic being. The ego is thus an islet on the sea of consciousness which in its turn is an islet on the boundless sea of the unconscious.

Pursuing these relations further we find that lying next

[1] The summaries of Jung's psychology given throughout this essay have been made from Jung's own writings (translated and untranslated). They also include definitions given by Jacobi in the *Psychology of Jung* (1943). Authoritative publications by Hinkle, Long, Baynes, G. Adler and others have also been consulted.

[2] There seems to be some confusion between the concept of the ego as presented by Jung and that outlined by some of his followers. Jung insists that the ego is purely conscious though he sometimes would like to break this rule. Jacobi says it is not exclusively conscious but is a *centre of reference* for conscious and unconscious psychic contents alike. And since Jung maintains first, that the conscious system results from a prior unconscious psyche, second, that the ego was born in the conscious mind and, third, that the ego 'turns its back' on the unconscious

24

to the conscious system is the Personal Unconscious. As distinct from the Collective Unconscious which is innate the Personal Unconscious is acquired. It consists of repressed, neglected and unapprehended elements. In an endeavour to correlate these concepts with the terms 'pre-conscious' and 'sub-conscious' which are freely but often inaccurately employed by psychologists at large, Jacobi states that the 'pre-conscious' (and here she means the Freudian pre-conscious) corresponds to that part of the Jungian Personal Unconscious which faces consciousness. Under the heading of the 'sub-conscious' (a term which from the first Freud explicitly rejected as meaning little more than pre-conscious but which many psychologists erroneously assume to be identical with Freud's dynamic 'unconscious') Jacobi includes 'unrecalled, unintended and unnoticed matters'. This 'sub-conscious', in the Jungian reckoning, lies between the fully conscious and the Collective Unconscious. Presumably therefore the pre-conscious is that part of the Jungian Personal Unconscious which faces consciousness and the 'sub-conscious' (as defined above) is that part of the Personal Unconscious which faces the Collective Unconscious. In other words the 'sub-conscious' can be identified more or less with the Personal Unconscious of Jung, not with Jung's Collective Unconscious.

Turning now to the Collective Unconscious we discover that this includes content not specific for the individual or acquired through individual experience but content acquired from the inherited possibility of psychic functioning in general, an inheritance common to all humanity. The Collective Unconscious is, however, divided into two regions,

----

mind it is clearly possible to have it both ways. Indeed Jung constantly toys with the notion that *another* ego exists in the unconscious but has little hope of finding it or at any rate of finding an order in the unconscious similar to that of ego-consciousness. Yet, he says, something must hold the unconscious together. 'Can it be', he asks, 'that the unconscious lost its centre when the ego was born?' Clearly then he does not *want* to make the ego partly unconscious. He wants two counterbalancing entities.

the first and nearest to the Personal Unconscious is a region of emotions, affects and primitive drives capable to some extent of rational control. Behind or below this or, to use another expression, at the obscure centre of the Collective Unconscious, are contents possessing elemental force, eternally incomprehensible and never to be assimilated fully by the ego. *The centre of the core can never be made conscious* although more superficially placed content and emotions can erupt into consciousness, as in the neuroses and psychoses and in the visions and hallucinations of creative spirits.

And here, leaving out of account for the moment such concepts (structures, functions or contents) as the *shadow*, the *anima* and *animus* and the *archetype*, we may pause to take stock. To a Freudian, contact with some of Jung's theoretical concepts is at first as bewildering as the experiences of Alice through the Looking-glass. The terms have a familiar ring, which is not surprising since some of them were originally coined by Freud; but they have come to mean something quite new and strange. The 'pre-conscious' part of Jung's Personal Unconscious is a region of subliminal contents waiting, so to speak, for the summons before they enter into consciousness. The deeper 'sub-conscious' on the other hand though still a part of the Personal Unconscious includes unrecalled, unintended and unnoticed matters lying between the fully conscious and the Collective Unconscious. Where exactly the repressed lies is not very clear. Apparently it lies mainly in the 'land of childhood' (a personal concept) where however it mingles with derivatives of the Collective Unconscious. The Jungian Personal Unconscious therefore includes the repressed but contains also matter that in the Freudian sense is capable of becoming conscious (the Freudian pre-conscious). Yet even the 'sub-conscious' layer of the Personal Unconscious which contains the repressed is distinct from the more important Collective Unconscious which presumably has some barrier of its own to separate its perpetually unconscious core from ego-consciousness. To judge however from the reference to repression of child memories, some mingling takes place at the more superficial levels. Nevertheless Jung's whole concept of the Personal Unconscious indicates that in his view it is a comparatively shallow system paling in significance before his all-powerful Collective Unconscious. And it may be noted in passing that Jung seeks, time and again, to identify this Personal Unconscious with the 'dynamic unconscious' of Freud, and thereby to divest the Freudian unconscious of its dynamic significance.

The complications that beset Jung's concepts are however best illustrated by reference to his ego theory. Certain dreams, visions and mystical experiences suggest to him the existence of a kind of consciousness in the unconscious. This would seem to involve the existence of an ego in the unconscious; and he is constantly on the watch for traces of a personality in the unconscious which he regards as intelligent and purposive, implying thereby that it takes cognizance. It is not clear whether Jung rejects the idea of a transcendental consciousness existing 'above' ego-consciousness, but he maintains that if it does exist its centre cannot be the human ego, which moreover being, according to Jung, essentially conscious is ineligible to function as a centre either to his Personal or his Collective Unconscious. Now if this means anything it means that he is uncertain whether there are not after all three types of dynamic ego (or at any rate ego traces) of which at least two can in their own way take cognizance, and at least one, existing in the Collective Unconscious, display intuition. The unconscious, he maintains, *personates*.

Although it is no part of my task to indicate ways out of the Jungian maze of structural concepts, I am tempted to suggest that the main source of confusion lies in Jung's neglect of the developmental factors that must inevitably play a part in the building up of his Personal Unconscious. As it stand the Jungian Personal Unconscious is indeed a lumber-room, to borrow Mr. Priestley's phrase. Alternatively the difficulty may be said to arise from the narrowness of

Jung's concept of the Ego and from his ambivalent reaction to the concept of an unconscious Ego. Both of these suggestions point to a third, namely, that the psychic structure of the *child's* mind is *terra incognita* to Jung who is clearly more at home either with schemata of the adult mind, which incidentally lend themselves readily to anthropomorphization, or with outlines of inaccessible psychic content that is either prehistoric or transcendental in nature. *Whatever may be the validity of these suggestions it is clear that the popular view according to which Jung's unconscious system is somehow broader or deeper than that of Freud is entirely fanciful. The concept of the dynamic unconscious originally advanced by Freud has been split up by Jung. One part has been assigned to a new container and branded with Jung's trade mark—the 'Collective Unconscious'. Another has been dissociated, reduced in dynamic significance and allocated to the Personal Unconscious. This latter superficial and mainly pre-conscious Jungian system is however represented as being Freud's whole stock-in-trade and returned to him labelled in a way calculated to mislead the uninformed.* Needless to say this transmogrification of Freud renders it extremely difficult to make any useful comparison between the systems of mental economics advanced respectively by Freud and by Jung. An organism with transposed organs cannot be expected to function according to the original plan. Under these circumstances the best we can do is to isolate these concepts which are not just transmogrified Freud and consider whether these purely Jungian contributions offer us any scientific premium that would justify their acceptance.

To return then to Jung's concept of the Collective Unconscious: we find that the qualifying term had originally a number of connotations. 'Collective', which would have been better represented by the term Racial, means also to him ideas common to the populace. At one point Jung tried to draw an analogy between the infant's (racial) 'knowing how' (to breathe, etc.), and racial 'knowing how' (to sym-

bolize, etc.). But generally speaking his Collective Unconscious is represented as being a thing of nature, neutral as
far as moral, aesthetic and intellectual judgements go. It is
like a collective human being having at its command a
human experience of a million years, a potential system of
psychic functioning handed down by generations of men, a
phylogenetic substructure of the modern mind. Whereas
conscious attitudes are directed by a Superior (in the sense
of predominating) Function which stands at the disposal of
the individual's conscious and belongs to the conscious
system, the Collective Unconscious is the repository of
Inferior (in the sense of unexercised) Functions. These include not only totally undifferentiated functions but functions which have through neglect or disuse sunk into the unconscious, presumably via the Personal Unconscious. There
they are entirely beyond the disposal of the individual's
will and apparently can cause a good deal of trouble.

To the exact nature of these Superior and Inferior
Functions, which, incidentally, comprise thinking, feeling,
intuition and sensation, we shall have occasion to return.
In the meantime we may note that Jung also uses the term
inferior to indicate less commendable qualities associated
with a person's uncontrolled emotional manifestations. The
existence of these morally and, it would seem also, function-
ally inferior qualities led Jung to formulate the concept of
the *shadow*. Regarding the exact nature of this structure,
Jung is rather reticent. He implies at some points, and
Jacobi supports the view, that the shadow can appertain to
ego-consciousness, to the Personal Unconscious and to the
Collective Unconscious. Yet Jung's main utterances on this
subject clearly indicate that, in his view, the shadow is a
variety of personality in the unconscious, indeed a focal
point of the Collective Unconscious.

It is sometimes difficult to distinguish Jung's *Shadow* from
that other personality which he finds in the unconscious and
which goes by the name of *anima* in the case of man and in
the case of woman *animus*. In the formation of both shadow

and anima sex factors (predispositions) seem to play a determining part. Thus the shadow of a man is masculine whereas his anima is feminine. Originally Jung freely identified the anima with the *soul*, by which he meant a personality reaction to the unconscious. Hence the anima came to be contrasted with the *persona* or personality reaction to the world of objects. The location of the anima was then rather uncertain: it could stand as a reaction system facing the Collective Unconscious or it could be part of the Collective Unconscious, indeed a focal part, a kind of personality in it. In later presentations uncertainty as to the status of the anima or animus continues. The animus represents the masculine elements in woman: the anima the feminine elements in man. The woman has several animi because woman is, consciously, the monogamous sex. On the same principle man, being polygamous, has but one anima. Yet, says Jung, since the Collective Unconscious is more than personal, so the anima is not always merely the feminine aspect of individual man. It has an archetypical aspect—the eternal feminine—which embodies an experience of woman far deeper than that undergone by the individual. Animus and anima, Jung remarks, are natural 'archetypes', primordial figures of the unconscious, and have given rise to the mythological gods and goddesses. Obviously, he says, they live or function in the deeper layers of the mind.

But what exactly does he mean by *archetypes*? According to Jung, these designate collective psychic content that has been subjected to no conscious treatment but represents an immediate psychic actuality, as in dreams and visions, to be distinguished from myths which are collective contents originally derived from the unconscious, but modified in a particular way and transmitted by esoteric teaching. Archetypes are patterns common to the whole of humanity, primordial types, images impressed on the mind since of old. They are, says Jacobi on Jung's behalf, 'representations of instinctive—i.e. psychologically necessary—responses to certain situations, which, circumventing consciousness, lead by virtue of their innate potentialities to behaviour corresponding to the psychological necessity even though it may not always appear appropriate when rationally viewed from without'. They do not, says Jung, consist of inherited ideas but of inherited predispositions to reaction. At the same time they are the organs of the soul. In the language of the unconscious, which is a picture language, the archetypes appear in personified or symbolized picture form. The myths of creation, the virgin birth, the forms of the snake, the Great Mother, the eternal feminine, Paradise, fourfoldness, the number three, all these are archetypical figures and formations of the Collective Unconscious.

It would be absurd to suggest that any psychological system can be condensed to a few paragraphs without doing some violence to its outline: nor, for the matter of that, is it possible to indicate by a few quotations the immense lather of verbosity in which Jung's concepts are smothered. From the point of view of scientific exposition Jung is at the best of times a confused writer, apparently unable to call a spade a spade and to keep on calling it a spade. Whether these peculiarities of style are due to the nature of his theories or to his own modes of thought is difficult to determine.[1] On many occasions he states quite frankly that he is anxious to avoid dogmatic theory; and the fact that he leaves all his ends untied may possibly account in part for the many inconsistencies and occasional evasions that mar his theoretical presentation. Nevertheless allowing for possible misunderstandings and the necessity of a rather condensed account, the foregoing résumé is accurate enough to permit some theoretical examination of his concept of the Collective

[1] Jung certainly manifests an uncontrollable propensity to pattern-making; and this is avowedly connected with his passion for the science of alchemy and, literally speaking, venerable numbers. Jacobi states not without pride that what sexuality is to Freud the number four is to Jung.

Unconscious and of the relations existing between its different parts and the ego.

Now when comparing different psychological systems it is essential to use common measures. Of these the most suitable is based on the premise that all mental activity is the result of changes, either qualitative or quantitative, in the state of mental energy. These changes are governed by three main factors, (a) 'constitutional', (b) 'predisposing' and (c) 'precipitating' or 'exciting'. The first is innate, the second developmental and the third immediate. It is from the interaction of these three factors that both normal and abnormal psychic manifestations acquire their characteristic form. Naturally most observers find it convenient to explain mental manifestations in terms of the third group, i.e., 'immediate' or 'exciting' causes, usually regarded as environmental in nature. Should this attempt miscarry their next step is to attribute the manifestations in question to 'constitutional' (innate) factors. Only when all other means have failed do they display a reluctant interest in 'developmental' factors 'predisposing' to normal or abnormal states. As a rule therefore it is easy to establish a direct ratio between the stress laid on constitutional and precipitating factors on the one hand and ignorance of developmental (individual) factors on the other.

Perhaps the best example of this state of affairs is afforded by pre-Freudian views of sexuality. In pre-Freudian times sexuality was held to originate at puberty; variations in sexual disposition and behaviour were regarded as exclusively constitutional. When Freud established that sexuality reaches an early peak of development at the age of five, it became clear that pubertal manifestations were decisively influenced by individual (predisposing) factors; and to that extent constitutional elements were scaled down to make way for individual elements. Similarly with other psychic manifestations. As knowledge of infantile stages in mental development increased, the importance of constitutional factors, and the particularity with which they were described, shrank rapidly until constitutional elements were ultimately described in vague terms as inherited tendencies or predispositions and thought of as acquiring immanence through the genes.

Now in so far as Jung is convinced of the overwhelming importance of the Collective Unconscious (and it must be remembered that although he appears to be sincerely convinced of this, he also adduces considerations which if correct would reduce its importance to the level of purely conscious forces and factors) he is clearly an ardent champion of the constitutional factor. And it is not without significance that his views regarding individual development factors are reactionary. Not only is Jung's Personal Unconscious a shallow system, but practically the whole of his clinical observations and aphorisms are concerned with the conscious or near-conscious reactions of adults. The fact that the mental development of infants and children can be mapped out in consecutive periods and that from month to month and from year to year the structure of mind becomes in both conscious and unconscious aspects increasingly complex, the fact that primitive infantile function is gradually overlapped by more sophisticated functions which though primitive enough are yet more adult than infantile, all this seems to have left Jung untouched and unconcerned. Indeed it is hard for any Freudian who takes the trouble to immerse his mind in Jungian psychology to avoid the horrid suspicion that Jung is nothing more or less than a pre-Freudian who having at first let himself be carried in the stream of Freudian thought has ever since striven to make his peace with conscious psychology.

This has happened time and again with Freudian schismatics. Breuer, quite frankly terrified by the deep waters in which he found himself, scrambled to the bank and abjured any further interest in dynamic psychology. There was indeed a certain handsomeness in Breuer's avowal of social and professional alarm. Other schismatics have followed other courses. Rank recanted his Freudian opinions and built a 'reactive psychology' in which all subsequent developments both normal and abnormal were correlated with variations in the experience of a 'birth trauma'. The recently developed Klein system of child psychology maintains that psychic development is governed by systems originating in the first six months of life. Although Adler made great play with environmental factors his 'will to power' is essentially a reaction to constitutional factors. Horney on the other hand abandoned dynamic psychology for a meticulous concern with the superficial rugosities of character. There are in fact three ways of attempting either implicitly or explicitly to negate Freudian views regarding unconscious function; first, to operate in terms of conscious or superficial pre-conscious psychology, second, to exaggerate the importance of constitutional or immediately post-natal factors and third, to give up psychology altogether.

Of these the most difficult to counter by scientific argument is the method of *emphasizing pre-structural elements* in psychic development. For there is a point in the investigation of infantile mental processes before which it is impossible to check theories by direct scientific examination of the material. That point is represented by the acquisition of the faculty to understand the meaning of verbally expressed ideas. In other words it is impossible to analyse children and therefore fully to explore their unconscious minds before the period when they can understand the analyst's interpretations. It is true the child's rudimentary speech and behaviour can be observed; but there are no means of checking the inferences as to unconscious function drawn by the observer from these data. The only criterion that can be applied to theories of early mental development is the extremely shaky one of plausibility. Herein I think lies the main attraction of the Jungian concept of the Collective Unconscious. Plausibility is a subjective factor. It is in any case hard enough to know what is going on in the mind of a two-year-old. A constant temptation exists to avoid the arduous task of individual research on sucklings by saying that what we don't know or can't understand is constitutional, the more so if this constitutional factor is decked out with 'content' that purports to represent in allegorical form the prehistory of the race. A romantical proceeding this, free from the tedious inconveniences and bafflements of nursery investigation.

But it would be manifestly unfair to suggest that Jung is nothing more than a psychological romantic. The idea that in psychic as in somatic affairs ontogeny repeats in blurred outline the story of phylogeny has stimulated many psychologists.[1] Its application to psychic affairs calls, however, for the closest discipline; and, other things being equal, preference should be given to explanations in terms of individual development. Admittedly we can infer the nature of unconscious processes only from direct and reported introspections; and psycho-biology compels us to assume the existence of constitutional variations; but at the very least we must examine the embryonic stages of individual development to see whether they could not account satisfactorily for those mental contents that led Jung to develop his theory of the collective or racial unconscious. Thus when considering the significance of Jung's archetypes, we must examine the primitive thinking processes of the child, in particular that archaic process that goes by the name of symbol formation.

Space does not permit any exhaustive account of the factors that influence early thought processes; amongst the more important are the concrete and predominantly visual nature of early mental presentations; the peculiar nature of those psychic tendencies or mechanisms (primary processes) which regulate unconscious function, in particular the mechanisms of condensation, displacement and identification; the rudimentary nature of early object relations; the predominating influence of early instinctual aims which, increased by frustration, leads to a constant projection on to the world of objects of characteristics really appertaining to

[1] Ontogeny=individual development; phylogeny=racial development.

the subject; and, finally, the influence of repression in maintaining a sharp distinction between the primary processes of the unconscious system and the secondary processes characteristic of the pre-conscious system, which system is in fact unable to expand until the development of word-presentation that follows the acquisition of speech and promotes intellectual activity. Baffling and often incomprehensible as are the products of early thinking they represent quite respectable achievements in concrete thought; indeed in the vast majority of instances it would be quite unnatural for the infant to think in any other way.

Admittedly it is never possible to observe these early products of unconscious thinking in pure form. Even in dream formation and in schizophrenic thinking the influence of the pre-conscious system on the final ideational representation is quite obvious. The latent content of a dream can only be recognized after it has been disentangled from a maze of (pre)conscious associations. Indeed a good deal of the intellectual obscurity of the dream is a direct consequence of the intrusion during sleep of primary processes into the field of the pre-conscious. A similar compounding (condensation) of primary and secondary processes is to be observed in the schizophrenic. During the profound mental regression which ushers in his disorder, he loses contact with the external objects of his instincts and substitutes a kind of dream contact with life. Hence the delusional and hallucinatory products which to the untrained observer seem so puzzling and so bizarre. But the schizophrenic never completely loses contact with his pre-conscious system. And, in fact, when he begins gradually to re-establish contact with life his first steps consist in playing with words rather than actual objects. The effect is for a long time just as bizarre as his hallucinatory and delusional regression. Only in the first few months of life can a state of mind exist which is governed exclusively by the primary processes. But, alas, we are not in a position to observe these directly.

To return to the Jungian archetypes; *the first and most*

striking feature of these products is the high degree of pre-conscious elaboration present in these largely pictorial representations. When Jung maintained that myth formations were 'elaborated' products, he unwittingly laid his concept of the collective archetype open to damaging criticism. For after a preliminary period when the child's most compelling needs are attended to by parents with a minimum of purposive activity on its own part, it is difficult to think of any instinctual contingency (need) that would not be interpreted by the child's mind in terms of its own experience, that is to say, thought of in terms of its current, *personal Weltanschauung*, which by the age of two includes a great deal of primitive wishful thinking and speculation. Also it must be remembered that in the embryonic phases of mental development no accurate sense of time exists even in the pre-conscious system (the unconscious is in any case timeless). The infant passes through many eternities before its rudimentary reality sense is organized, and during those endless epochs its mental activity waxes and wanes in accordance with the stress of need. Small wonder then if its earliest, pre-conscious speculative systems are stamped with the hallmark of unconscious thinking; that, for example, what the adult regards as a peculiar form of symbolism is to the child a matter of fact.

To reduce all this to more concrete terms: although up to the age of two the existence of 'collective archetypes' can neither be proved nor disproved, we are entitled to estimate the plausibility of such assumptions by reference to the forms of *individual* thinking, both conscious and unconscious, existing from the age of two onwards. Is it, for example, likely that the two-year-old's reactions to the objects of its instincts are influenced mainly by the collective archetype of the eternal feminine or mainly by 'eternities' of experience of instinctual need and gratification, pleasure and pain, and by the correlation of these experiences with the perception and gradual recognition of the chiefly maternal 'objects' which cater for and therefore appear responsible

37

for its well- or ill-being both physical and mental. Is it likely that the number two or three or four, or for that matter, five, six or seven, obtains its archetypical significance from the impinging of inherited psychic predisposition on the (pre)conscious system; or is it likely that the early significance of numbers (which cannot in any case develop until the infant has attained the transitional period that lies between mainly visual and mainly auditory thinking, by which time the (pre)conscious system is already well advanced) is due to the influence of the 'individual' unconscious system on early pre-conscious thinking? On questions of this sort a good deal of evidence has been collected. We know, for example, that by the time the child is thumbing its first rag picture-book and learning that 'b' stands for 'ball', it has already invested the letters of the alphabet with symbolic significance, that, for example, in its mind 'b' may symbolize its mother and 'd' its father; and there is overwhelming evidence that behind this symbolism lies a wealth of individual experience of both father and mother, experience of the primitive relations between subject and object that has undergone extensive if, to the adult, peculiar organization.

To these individual factors we shall have occasion to return. *In the meantime it may be said not only that many Jungian archetypes are capable of adequate explanation in terms of purely individual thought but also that so long as we have not fully explored the early forms of individual thinking, the validity and universality of the collective archetype is under strong suspicion.* It is, of course, still arguable that inherited psychic predispositions express themselves through whatever form of individual organization may have developed; but that is not the same thing as a collective archetype in Jung's sense of the term. And in any case the law of economy of hypothesis would demand that the term should be applied only to such products as cannot be satisfactorily accounted for in terms of individual development.

As a matter of interest, it was through the application of this criterion that Freud was originally led to formulate some tentative views regarding the inheritance of certain racial psychic dispositions and more specifically the inheritance of racial memory traces; views which have led many psychologists to the erroneous conclusion that in his latter days Freud found himself nearer to the Jungian concept of the Collective Unconscious. This was far from being the case. Freud was always interested in the primitive factors that play a part in inducing and regulating mental activities. This was a natural outcome of his discovery of the unconscious system and of the primitive instincts and mechanisms that respectively activate and govern that system. To these concepts he added the corollary of an 'instinctual disposition' capable of giving rise to characteristic mental patterns either positive (the result of inherent instinctual tendencies or aims) or reactive (the result of the impact of these tendencies on characteristic social restrictions). And it may be noted in passing that he saw no particular advantage in calling these constitutional dispositions 'collective'; for, as he remarked, 'the content of the unconscious is in any case collective, a general possession of mankind'. In other words the qualifying term adds nothing to our information.

Freud was also keenly interested in certain clinical types found particularly amongst the hysterical and obsessional neuroses suggesting the existence of an *archaic* disposition and even the possibility of inherited mental residues. The most striking example in his view, was that primitive character type manifesting a violent degree of ambivalence.[1] This he at first regarded as evidence of a persisting disposition, i.e., of reaction traits once characteristic of primitive man. Following this idea he proceeded to correlate neurotic symptoms with the persistence of reactions that were universal in primeval times. In *Totem and Tabu* (1912) he first drew attention to the correspondence existing between certain neurotic (obsessional) rituals and the totemistic observances followed by primitive tribes. From that time

[1] The coexistence or fusion of opposing tendencies, e.g., of love and hate, usually vented on the objects of instincts.

onward he maintained that religious phenomena were to be understood only on the model of neurotic symptoms as a return of long-forgotten important happenings in the primeval history of the human family. This view he supported from the observation that the unconscious sexual anxieties of children were accompanied by reactions which seem unreasonable in the individual (cf. infantile phobias of being eaten or castrated and phantasies of a 'primal scene' of sadistic coitus between the parents during which the child's life and sexual organs are felt to be endangered). In the absence of individual traumatic experiences these, he maintained, can only be understood phylogenetically. In *Moses and Monotheism* (1939) he returned to the subject. Studying the history of mass-traditions he again concluded that in the development of religious phenomena a state of affairs exists corresponding to the 'return of the repressed' observed in individual neuroses; and he asserted that 'the archaic heritage of mankind includes not only archaic dispositions but also ideational contents, memory traces of the experience of former generations'. Freud realized fully that the present attitude of biological science rejects the idea of acquired qualities being transmitted to descendants. Nothing daunted by this opposition, he maintained that he was unable to picture biological development without taking this into account.

In further support of the idea of an archaic heritage of ideational content representing phylogenetic 'fragments', Freud adduced the case of symbolism. This he regarded as an archaic inheritance from the time when primitive man painfully acquired the power of speech. He admitted nevertheless that symbolism was capable of another explanation, namely, that symbols are thought-connexions between ideas formed during the historical development of speech which have to be repeated every time the individual passes through his infantile development, implying thereby that only the thought disposition was inherited. In the case of mass-psychology, however, he was definitely of the opinion that

40

mental residues of primeval times need only to be awakened not reacquired.

For the moment we are not concerned with the accuracy or validity of these views. As has been indicated, until the child is able to communicate ideas (i.e. after the age of two years) we have no means of testing by interpretation the accuracy of any theory regarding the nature of unconscious content. We can neither prove nor disprove the inheritance of psychic memory traces. All we can say is that with increasing understanding (drawn of course from a number of collateral sources) of the mental function of two-year-olds we shall in all probability find that many apparently unreasonable infantile reactions are amply accounted for without assuming more than the inheritance of instinctual dispositions, of sensitiveness of psychic reaction and of thought dispositions. The immediate issue is quite otherwise, namely, whether these views of Freud represent an acceptance on his part of Jung's concept of the Collective Unconscious and of its content, meaning and function. For naturally acceptance of constitutional (innate) factors is not peculiar either to Jung or to Freud.

The simplest answer is that the analogy Freud drew between, on the one hand, neurotic symptom formations occurring in the individual and, on the other, religious phenomena appearing in the mass, and the correlations he made between both of these manifestations and traumatic events occurring in the primeval history of man, were entirely consonant with his own theories of individual mental development and function, theories which Jung had both explicitly and implicitly rejected, and which he continues to reject even when, by using Freudian terminology in a non-Freudian sense and by occasional suggestions that Freud's view might be right for some people sometimes, he appears to indicate condescendingly that he is not totally opposed to Freudian conceptions. Following his correlation of neurotic reactions with the occurrence of early psychic traumata acting on a sensitive constitution, Freud maintained that the

41

inherited phylogenetic fragments referred only to events of catastrophic (traumatic) significance occurring in primeval times and concerned, not with allegorical abstractions, but with the concrete development of the human family. The events in question represented a combination of sexual and aggressive elements, e.g., the murder of the primal father, or the development of a taboo on incest, which in one way or another were associated with serious threats to the survival of man. The effect of these traumata varied quantitatively and also in accordance with environmental stresses, and was enhanced by the factor of summation, i.e., the situations were repeated over many centuries of human experience. In fact Freud drew an exact parallel between the primeval conditions inducing racial traumata and the psychic and environmental conditions giving rise to infantile neuroses.

Similarly the conditions giving rise to symbol formation were strictly limited. Although the number of symbols runs into thousands, the unconscious ideas represented in symbols are confined to a small number of primitive interests concerning the subject's own body, family figures and the phenomena of birth, sexuality and death. By far the greatest number are sexual. They are based on primitive identifications, represent a compromise between the repressed and repressing tendencies, are always concrete and represent regressions to simpler forms of apprehension. Moreover the track of true symbolism is a one-way track from the unconscious to the pre-conscious. Thus while the phallus is symbolized by a snake, the snake is never symbolized by the phallus. Contrary to the views held by Jung, the symbol is regarded not as a concrete representation of an abstract idea but as a concrete representation of a more inaccessible idea, i.e., the snake represents the phallus not just power, virility or sexuality.[1] Nor is there any 'higher' idea implicit in the

[1] By far the most weighty and authoritative account of symbolism is given by Ernest Jones in his article 'The Theory of Symbolism' (*Papers on Psycho-analysis*, 1949).

symbolism; on the contrary, the unconscious derivatives present in the symbol formation act as an obstacle to the development of more realistic representations. Whether Freud's view that symbols represent phylogenetic traces is accurate or whether, as many Freudian analysts prefer to think, symbols are re-created in the course of individual development, the fact remains that there is no resemblance between these formations and the mystical representations of the Collective Unconscious described by Jung as archetypes.

But the most convincing evidence that no approximation of concepts occurred to bridge the gulf between Freudian and Jungian systems lies in the fact that despite Freud's obvious interest in the psycho-biological aspects of the constitutional factor, *these were at all times subordinated to his concern with the unconscious aspects of individual development*. The whole structure of Freudian metapsychology is unaffected by his incursion into the region of phylogenetic speculation. Nor is there a vestige of truth in the suggestion that in formulating the concept of the Id, Freud laid the foundation for a *rapprochement* with Jungian systems. On the contrary the concept of the Id strengthened immeasurably Freud's outline of the mental apparatus and led to the development of an ego-psychology in which the complications of early mental development could be adequately represented. All primary instincts start in the Id from which the Ego itself develops. As a result of Ego exertions, part of the Id can be raised to the pre-conscious level. Other parts are not so raised and remain to form the true unconscious. Should Id charges threaten the security of the Ego, even those parts that have secured preconscious representation can once more be lowered to Id levels by repression. Traumata tend to remain at unconscious levels and if reactivated are subject to repression. Finally the constitutional factor operates through the Id towards the Ego. By establishing the Id-concept Freud was able to preserve and strengthen the elaborate series of discoveries regarding *the unconscious*

43

development of the individual which constitute his un-paralleled contribution to mental science.

And here I think we may add to the practical criteria of assessment outlined earlier. A satisfactory psychological system must be able not only to account for the complications of mental development: it must hang together. If it is not to be dismissed as a series of improvisations it must *be* systematic. Save where the data of observation indicate the existence of contradictions inherent in mental functioning, it must not contain too many contradictions. And finally it must be able to describe a hierarchy of functions in keeping with the recognized stages of psycho-biological development of man. In summing up the structural aspects of Jung's psychological systems, we are entitled therefore to ask whether they hang together, whether they involve too many contradictions and whether in fact they have psycho-biological value.

The last of these criteria is by far the most fundamental. Whether they know it or not dynamic psychologists have saddled themselves with weighty responsibilities. Either explicitly or implicitly they have committed themselves to the view that the structure of mind arises from the psycho-biological need to regulate mental forces, indicating thereby that the overriding factor in mental activity is a dynamic one. In this respect the problem of the dynamic psychologist is identical with that of humanity, namely, to discover ways and means whereby primitive forces can be regulated without damaging man's capacity to adapt to his natural surroundings or to the social environment he has created through his group activities. Whatever theories of mental development and function the dynamic psychologist may advance must not violate his central hypothesis that the most powerful of all the psychic systems is that which harbours man's instinctual forces. Obviously it would be inconsistent with this hypothesis to maintain at the same time that superficial institutions or mental instruments or functions can bring about spontaneously profound changes in the deepest unconscious systems. The dynamic psychologist cannot have it both ways.

44

Now it is only fair to Jung to record that at the outset of his psychological career he was an enthusiastic dynamic psychologist. In point of fact his first direct contact with unconscious psychology was made some twelve years *after* Freud had discovered the unconscious and had described his theory of neuroses and of dream formation. Jung, who was then working at Burghölzli as first assistant to Bleuler, took part under Bleuler's direction in a team investigation intended to test Freud's theories, in particular the existence of infantile sexuality. The late Dr. Brill of New York who ranked high amongst clinical psychologists as a man of scientific integrity has described how on his arrival at Zürich in 1907 he found that the staff had been enthusiastically engaged in this work for about a year.[1] In the light of Jung's later defection, Brill's comments on Jung's attitude are of some significance: 'Jung was the first assistant and at the same time a very ardent and pugnacious Freudian', . . . (he) 'gave the impression that he was fully convinced of everything (Freudian)', '. . . you could not express any doubt about Freud's views without arousing his ire'.

To the clinical psychologist it is not altogether surprising therefore to find that within a few years Jung recanted his Freudian views and devoted his professional life to the promulgation of theories and systems which had they been accurate would have completely disembowelled the Freudian system. For despite Jung's occasional condescending admissions of a 'limited' applicability of Freudian theories, *his own system is persistently if not consistently anti-Freudian.* Indeed it is characteristic of Freudian schismatics that they do not rest content until they have produced a theoretical structure which denies the validity of the most fundamental of Freud's discoveries, at the same time using Freudian terminology in a way that divests it of its original meaning and so bamboozles the unoriented reader. There are, of course, two ways of supplanting Freudian theories. The less common is to elaborate systems which imply that Freud was super-

[1] *Psycho-analytic Psychiatry.* 1948.

ficial: the other and more common technique is to reinforce the authority of those *conscious* psychologies whose sway Freud had so uncompromisingly disturbed. Jung elected to follow both plans.

Actually Jung's claim to be regarded as a dynamic psychologist now rests on a cult of the Collective Unconscious. This he regards as the most important of his psychic systems; its unguarded emergence can, he maintains, cause the gravest psychotic disorders; in the sense of giving rise to specific content it has a fixed organization; it is the repository of the wisdom of the past which is apparently wiser than anything ego-consciousness can produce unaided, it is a 'dreamer of age-old dreams', an 'incomparable prognosticator' and 'could be personified as an almost (*sic*) immortal human being with characteristics of both sexes, transcending youth and age, birth and death . . . .' In language of this sort Jung proclaims himself not only a dynamic psychologist but a dynamic psychologist with a unique perception of the 'dark' and 'deep' forces that influence human affairs. Yet it is precisely by his undisciplined use of language that Jung gives a clue to the fundamental flaw in his psychological reasoning. Whoever anthropomorphizes the dynamic unconscious has failed to distinguish between primary and secondary mental processes and has thereby obliterated the distinction between unconscious and pre-conscious systems. Indeed he has done more; he has paved the way for an introduction into the unconscious system of concepts that are valid only for ego-consciousness. *And so almost in the same moment as he proclaims himself a champion of a unique dynamic unconscious Jung reveals himself in his true colours as a conventional almost academic conscious psychologist.* Once he has outlined the Collective Unconscious and postulated its immeasurable force, his main concern is to establish that the relation of this powerful system to the conscious system is that of a mutual improvement association. The Collective Unconscious, it would appear, ripens (however slowly) with experience; a compensatory relation exists between the conscious and the

46

unconscious: the existence of one set of attitudes in the conscious system calls out or is balanced by an antithetical set in the Collective Unconscious; inferior functions that have been neglected by ego-consciousness sink into the unconscious where, reinforcing functions that have never been developed, they exert an influence on the conscious system that is beyond the control of will. 'The complementary or compensatory functions to each other', says Jacobi, 'is a law inherent in the structure of the psyche.' And again: 'If consciousness is extraverted, the unconscious is introverted (*sic*), and conversely.' And despite a good deal of lip-service to generalizations such as that the conscious system arises from the matrix of the unconscious, Jung's whole outline of the development of the individual substitutes for an evolutionary approach from unconscious to conscious and a sharp differentiation of an originally dynamic unconscious from later structural formations, a closed system of interrelations, compensations, balances and antitheses which cut the ground from under that fundamental distinction.

Seeking for a Jungian concept which at the same time illustrates the flattening out of distinctions between his unconscious and his conscious systems, brings into prominence the contradictions inherent in his psychological thinking and focuses attention on its main flaw, one cannot do better than choose the *anima* and *animus*(*-i*). For quite frankly it is impossible to operate with such metapsychologically nebulous concepts as the *shadow*, or indeed with any concept that requires for its elucidation the use of terms such as 'light' and 'dark', the 'light side' and the 'dark side', 'this side' and 'the other side', 'the shadowy side' and the like. The *anima*(*-us,-i*) concept is after all not only a focal point in the Jungian collective unconscious, it is an essential part of his total system; it has been expounded at great length by Jung and his followers; and, apart from difficulties arising from his use of the term as a synonym for the Jungian 'soul', it is possible to subject it to a partial examination.

47

Now it may be noted that, although Jung seeks to correlate the concepts of the anima and animus with the transmission of genes and therefore with the problem of bisexu-
ality, this biological consideration is not consistently applied
and gives place to a maze of, e.g., so-called 'contra-sexual'
relationships. On the assumption that unconscious and
conscious relations are governed by opposites, the anima(-us,
-i) is rather ingeniously represented as the 'contra-sexual
position' of the individual, a kind of 'minority representation', in the case of man of his feminine side, in the case of
woman of her masculine side or tendencies. It is also,
however, a precipitate of *all* human experience pertaining
to the 'other' sex. But here as elsewhere in Jung's writings it
may be noted that the sexual factor is definitely not nasty.
The anima(-us, -i), represents not crude sexual elements
but rather what might be called *tertiary* sexual characteristics, refined and elevated to an archetypical plane from
which nevertheless it may on occasion exercise an influence
sufficiently potent to disrupt the psyche. In general the
anima is viewed as the mysterious, veiled female form, a
kind of idealized, sometimes admonitory figure of the type,
Jung suggests, of Dante's Beatrice or Rider Haggard's
'She'. Sometimes she is a poor weak woman who may in
dreams get mixed up with a wife image, or, in waking life,
be projected on to a real woman with unfortunate results.
The *animi* of the woman, for as we have seen women being
monogamous have a plurality of animi, bear a strong like-
ness to father images or Wise *Old* Men. Now here we are
plunged into all possible sorts of confusion; for if this plurality of figures represent 'objects' as would appear from their
polygamous function why are they not women rather than
'father-figures'? Granted that by Jung's refined categories
the masculine side of a woman represents only her 'higher'
potentialities, e.g., fitness for a career or for 'inner' development, we may still ask why is not this unconscious masculine
side homosexual? Surely this would fit in with the compen-
48

sating relation existing between the *animus* and the conscious personality.[1]

But the confusion does not end here. According to Jung, and here Dr. G. Adler lends his authoritative support, the unconscious is feminine, the conscious masculine, irrespective of the sex of the individual: '. . . the feminine and masculine psychic powers, the unconscious and conscious poles of the personality' says Adler, 'are united in a psychic totality to which—to use the language of alchemy—we could apply the symbol of the hermaphrodite'. Moreover thinking is masculine, feeling is feminine. The Inferior Function being unconscious must be feminine, Superior Function masculine; 'Eros' (*sic*) is feminine: 'Logos' masculine. The *soul*, everybody's soul, is feminine. Yet the man's shadow which is mainly an unconscious personality is masculine: the shadow of a woman feminine. It is tempting to join in this fun. The Unconscious being older and more comprehensive than the Conscious should be superior and therefore one might think masculine. The anima can be the dream representative of man's unconscious feminine side. But surely every man has some conscious glimmer of his feminine side;

[1] It is interesting to speculate as to the ultimate fate of the *anima* (*-us*) concept, for like many of Jung's concepts it appears to exist in a state of flux. At times one gets the impression that it is a favourite plaything which might later on be discarded: at times it appears to drift steadily away from its shaky moorings as a scientific concept, i.e., a 'psychic partial-system' personifying, according to the definition of the moment, affective experiences, the 'contra-sexual' or the unconscious in general. The drift towards occult thought is well illustrated in Jung's commentary on *The Secret of the Golden Flower* by *Lu Tzu*. Jung accepts Wilhelm's translation of the word *hun* as *animus* and of *p'o* as *anima*. The *animus*, according to *Lu Tzu*, 'lives in the daytime in the eyes: at night it houses in the liver. When living in the eyes it sees; when housing itself in the liver, it dreams'. Here Jung comments, 'none the less I had very important reasons for choosing the expression *logos* for a man's mental essence, his clarity of consciousness and reason'. Regarding *p'o*, he remarks 'Careful investigation has shewn that the affective character in a man has feminine traits. From this psychological fact comes the Chinese teaching of the *p'o*-soul, as well as my concept of the *anima*'.

49

if so, this should be reversed to masculine in the unconscious. If the conscious is masculine and the unconscious feminine, then by the Jungian rule of contraries, the anima should oppose the conscious. But she only represents the 'sexual minority', and should therefore appear as a masculine figure in an otherwise feminine unconscious. Or again, suppose a man's Inferior Function to be the Thinking Function: as inferior and unconscious it is *ex hypothesi* feminine. But thinking, we are told, is masculine. At what point does this metamorphosis take place?

It would be easy to account for these confusions by saying that they are due in part to Jung's doting attitude to alchemy and oriental occultism, in part to a desire to present mystical ideas in a 'modern' scientific guise; witness his references to genes. And no doubt the absurdities are also due to some extent to the constant interference of random thinking. More significant, however, are the specific tendencies expressed by the structure of the Jungian system. Two in particular may be singled out. By establishing a series of intimate, spontaneously developed and *reciprocal* relationships between structures of the unconscious and of the conscious, Jung in effect obliterates the dynamic distinction between the two systems; and by his emphasis on the archetypical aspects of the Collective Unconscious, he deliberately sidesteps the major problem of infantile sexuality and its profound influence on mental development. This is too big a price to pay for the questionable benefits of a drawing-room version of psychic development.

All of which leads to a final psycho-biological consideration. Reviewing the archetypical aspects of the anima one cannot help wondering why a structure that has such terrifying potentiality is represented as being so polite, platonic and Tennysonian. And, going further, we may inquire why the whole content of the Collective Unconscious is so wise, wonderful and precious. Why is the 'old' so venerable? Above all, why is it so experienced? A prehistoric human skull reposing in a museum is no doubt enormously old. It may even be enormously interesting. But it is not particularly venerable. In point of fact the former contents of the skull, or, to speak in psychological terms, the mind of that prehistoric man, must have been immeasurably younger than the mind of modern man. It must indeed have had less racial unconscious to provide it with 'wisdom'. The racial unconscious is no more old than a baby is old. Its conceivably 'transmissible' tendencies can hardly be supposed to grow at all. How can an inherited *tendency* acquire wisdom and experience? We cannot talk of wisdom until instinctual urges and unconscious content have been refracted through the reality layers of the (pre-)conscious system. Wisdom grows with the development of conceptual forms which depend in turn on word-formation and the power of speech, faculties which are associated mainly with the pre-conscious function. So far from being particularly wise the archetypes are of a predominantly superstitious and animistic nature. The forms of symbolism are also archaic, naive and from the point of view of reality function profoundly obscurantist. Indeed we are still struggling with some of the legacies of anxiety, cruelty and cowardice left us by our primitive forefathers. No doubt we have lost the faculty of throwing coconuts from treetops with precision, but our experience is nevertheless incomparably greater than that of our simian ancestors.

The truth appears to be that Jung in pursuance of his witting or unwitting policy of levelling distinctions between the unconscious and the conscious confuses archetypes with traditions. His whole system of structural concepts illustrates the dangers of thinking of the psyche in symbolical terms. Indeed it could be maintained that the concept of a wise and venerable Collective Unconscious owes its development to the persistence of a myth. For although it would not be quite accurate to say that Jung's account of its virtues and powers indicates his belief in the myth of a Golden Age of Man, there is some reason to think that the concept of the Collective Unconscious resuscitates that sentimental derivative of ancestor worship, the Myth of the Noble Savage.

51

CHAPTER III

MENTAL ENERGY

IT cannot be repeated too often that the body of psycho-analytical knowledge regarding the function of mind which Freud latterly designated as 'metapsychology' was acquired through the application of three different methods of conceptual approach; structural or topographic, dynamic and economic. No mental event can be adequately understood unless these three methods are applied to the data of observation and introspection. Whoever conceives of mind in the structural sense as an *apparatus* or *instrument* is under obligation to concede or at any rate to conceive the existence of mental *energy* which sets this apparatus in motion. And no sooner has he made this concession than he is faced with the necessity of describing the *mechanisms* by means of which this energy is *distributed* through the various systems of which the mental apparatus is composed. This further obligation imposes certain conditions on any formulation of the concept of mental energy. For although caution and the law of economy of hypothesis would dictate that the concept of psychic energy be stated in the most sparing terms, yet the account must be sufficiently circumstantial to explain variations in mental function.

To postulate, as some psychologists do, as many as a hundred primary instincts, is to reduce psycho-dynamics to a parlour game; to refuse to make any distinction between primary instincts is equally stultifying. Even the terms used to designate mental energy are subject to this condition. One may describe psychic energy as *élan vital* or as the spirit of God or one may take refuge in a non-committal symbol and talk of ψ-energy, but in the long run the usefulness of the term adopted will depend on the light it throws on both the somatic and the psychic functions of man.

Now it is scarcely profitable to compare or contrast the

concepts of psychic energy used by Freud and by Jung unless one bears in mind the historical development of each concept. It is often urged against Freudian theories that they were derived from a study of the abnormal. Yet looking back over the history of psycho-analysis it is clear that without Freud's discovery of *unconscious conflict* sufficiently violent to give rise to mental disease, dynamic psychology would have been stillborn, or at any rate would not have passed the descriptive stages outlined, for example, by McDougall. Examination of the unconscious conflict responsible for the psycho-neuroses led Freud to the discovery that the sexual instincts do not, as had previously been imagined, originate at puberty, but can be traced back to infancy and comprise a number of primitive sexual components derived from various 'erotogenic' body zones, e.g. oral, anal, cutaneous, muscular and (infantile) genital. These component instincts are at first loosely organized and only later pass under the primacy of genital impulses. It was also observed that these infantile components of sexuality can be fused with aggressive and destructive impulses giving rise to various forms of sadism; these are named after the sexual component with which they are associated, e.g. oral and anal sadism. To express this in more descriptive terms: Freud discovered that during infancy and early childhood a rapid development of sexual instincts takes place. These draw their energies from widely scattered bodily sources and, apart from those components which can be gratified on the child's own body, are directed towards the parents or their most important substitutes. Once the component instincts come under the primacy of the infantile genital zones, the aim of the infant's sexuality is to obtain genital gratification on parental objects. This represents the Oedipus phase of development which reaches its height between the third and the fifth year of life. The degree to which these incestuous drives obtain conscious expression in thought, word or action depends partly on the inhibitory forces directed by the parents against the child's early sexual strivings and partly on internal restrictions.

53

Internal obstacles are set up because of (*a*) the unconscious anxiety of sexual mutilation (punishment) and (*b*) the guilt induced by the jealousy, rivalry and hatred that inevitably accompany primitive sexual striving and follow its frustration.

But, despite the discovery of infantile sadism and of the sexual rivalry that canalizes it in the direction of parental objects who are also loved, the importance of the aggressive instincts was not clearly recognized at this stage of investigation. Conflict was thought of as an opposition between the aims of sexual instincts and those of non-sexual (ego) instincts, including in particular the impulses of self-preservation. Partly for this reason psycho-analytical attention was focused mainly on the forms of sexual energy to which Freud applied the term *libido*. More detailed investigations were soon to lead to further extension of this term. Not only could a distinction be drawn between *libido directed towards sexual objects* and *libido that can be gratified on the self* (auto-erotic impulses) but it became clear that the ego itself is the repository of large quantities of libido that are not diverted to external objects. This concept of *narcissistic* or *ego-libido* was further extended to include libido investing the body organs in general, which was then referred to as *organ* or *body libido*. And here for a time the matter rested.

The next stage in the development of Freudian theories of instinct arose from study of the ego-disorders present in various forms of insanity. Manifestations such as delusions of grandeur had already indicated the vital part played by narcissistic or ego-libido in regressive ego-disorder; these inflations of the ego are initiated by a withdrawal of libido from external objects which gives rise to a pathological increase in narcissistic libido. The now excessive charges of libido within the ego stimulate feelings of grandiosity which may reach delusional intensity. This finding was subsequently corroborated by investigation of the traumatic neuroses of war. To superficial inspection war-neuroses appear to be due to the threat to self-preservation existing under combatant conditions, but closer examination shows that two specific factors are responsible for these disorders, first, the disturbance of narcissistic libido caused by war-traumata and, second, the incapacity of the individual to endure the mobilization of aggressive instincts inseparable from war conditions. From yet another source came convincing evidence that disturbance in the distribution of aggressive energies and of narcissistic libido was decisive for ego-disorder. Freud's study of melancholia, which is essentially a malignant disease of the unconscious conscience, proved conclusively that when libidinal relations with the world of objects are fundamentally disturbed and when libido is withdrawn from these objects, not only does the narcissistic libido of the individual become pathologically overcharged but quantities of aggressive energy are freed with which the mind is unable to cope. Under normal circumstances aggressive impulses freed in this way are turned on the self and for the most part canalized through the critical activities of unconscious conscience, their aggressive aim being however held in check by the existence of a healthy narcissism. The diseased narcissism of the melancholiac is unable to provide this defence and the result is a diminution of vital psychic activity varying in degree from apathy to that state of narcissistic disorder where inturned aggression triumphs in the act of suicide.

This extension of the idea of mental conflict to include disturbances in the balance of libidinal and of aggressive energies compelled Freud to recast his previous formulations regarding mental dynamics, a task which he faced unflinchingly. The concept of specific ego-instincts was discarded and the function of the ego as a 'psychic regulator' was expanded. The impulses of self-preservation were regarded as one of a group of Life-instincts varying only in the degree of their lability. *The fundamental psychic antithesis was no longer between the libido and ego-instincts but between all forms of libidinal energy (the Erotic Instincts, in the sense given by Plato to* Eros *in his* Symposium) *and the instincts of*

aggression or destruction. For purposes of theoretical presentation Freud postulated a Death-instinct of which the most
obvious manifestation is aggression directed either towards
the world of objects or towards the ego.[1] This dualistic conception of the primary instinctual forces had always been
implicit in the concept of conflict. Freud's final formulations
had merely indicated that from its earliest beginnings the
ego is a battle-ground for primitive instinctual conflicts.[2]
Throughout his investigations of this fundamental problem,
Freud was constantly guided by psycho-biological principles
as well as by clinical exigencies. He not only extended the
concept of libido but described with circumstantiality the
various modifications it undergoes *during individual development.* Correlating these findings with a parallel series of
discoveries regarding the vicissitudes of aggression, he was
able to establish *conflict-formulæ* reflecting different stages
of mental development and appropriate to different varieties
of mental disorder. At the same time he solved the problem
of the classification of instincts: for clearly only those instincts can be regarded as primary, frustration of which is
able to disrupt the normal function of mind.

To turn now to Jung: it is not at all clear, nor in the

[1] A good deal of the opposition to Freud's theory of a Death-instinct
is due to a misunderstanding of his use of the term 'death'. Freud's
dynamic concept of instinct led him to regard it as an inherent tendency to reinstate a pre-existing condition: the Death-instinct is thus a
tendency inherent in animate matter to return to the inanimate state,
not, as is often thought, an individual (ego) longing for death. Even if
the concept of a Death-instinct were discarded, the instinctual antithesis of aggression and love would remain firmly based on clinical
observation.

[2] It was during his investigation of melancholia that Freud was able
to establish the structural aspects of unconscious conflict. The ego being
threatened with the excitations of unmodified instinct gradually develops a specialized ego-institution, the function of which is to detect
mounting charges of primitive instinct and to instigate appropriate
ego-defences. This *super-ego*, or unconscious conscience, which is
modelled on experiences of the scrutinizing and inhibiting activities of
parents, constitutes in fact a parental institution within the mind.

present writer's opinion is it likely ever to become clear from
Jung's writings, why, having originally committed himself,
whether he knew it or not, to Freud's dualistic theories of
instinctual conflict, Jung embraced with such enthusiastic
haste a monistic theory of mental energy. Jung himself
offers a clinical and in that sense therefore a potentially
scientific explanation. Although ready to concede that the
Freudian libido played *some* part in the development of
adult neuroses, he came to the conclusion that the Freudian
libido theory did not explain the ego regressions and delusional products of dementia praecox (schizophrenia). One
cannot but surmise from this that Jung had never really
grasped Freud's concept of the libido and that he continued
wittingly or unwittingly to equate it with the energy of
adult sexual instincts. Only on this assumption can we account for Jung's blindness to the facts of infantile sexuality
and his total neglect of the concept of narcissistic libido. A
moment's consideration should have shown that the conflict
present in dementia praecox necessitated an expansion
rather than a contraction of the Freudian libido concept.
The more profound the disturbance the sharper the conflict
and the more primitive the energies (instincts) involved. As
the spontaneous remissions occurring in even advanced states
of insanity clearly indicate, the fault in reality-testing that
permits the development of hallucinations and delusions is
due not to an essential defect in the intellectual apparatus
but, in the first instance, to the withdrawal of libidinal
energy (using this term in the Freudian sense) from relations
with objects in the outer world, in the second place to a gross
disturbance of mental function due to the flooding of the
mental apparatus with dammed-up libido and in the third to
the inchoate and disordered efforts of this damaged apparatus
to regain contact with the world of objects (reality). Had any
reasonable doubt on these points remained, it could easily
have been dispelled by studying the gradual expansion of
'interest' manifested by infants during their early phases of
development. For during the period when reality needs are

to a large extent catered for by external (parental) objects, and when intellectual processes are of the most rudimentary order, it is plain to naked-eye observation that the infant's interest in its own body, in the existence of instinctual objects and in a variety of inanimate objects, is stimulated by the exercise of libidinal function (in the Freudian sense of the term). The simplest example is the displacement of breast interest to thumb-sucking and subsequently to a great variety of substitute-objects of a 'comforter' type. Nevertheless, we must accept as his final pronouncement on the subject, Jung's monistic theory of mental energy, and are left with the task of stating its essential features.

Reading those of Jung's publications which appeared about the time of his defection from Freud, it is sometimes difficult to be sure whether Jung had really changed his mind or not. Despite categorical statements as to the monistic nature of mental energy he continued to talk of libido as if it behaved in the same way as the libido posited by Freud. Only in Jung's later writings does it become uncompromisingly clear that in his view libido is nothing more than a synonym for psychic energy. He insists, however, that libido is not a psychic *force* but rather the intensity of a psychic process, more specifically the psychological *value* of a psychic process, meaning by value not an imparted moral, aesthetic or intellectual value, but the determining power of a psychic process as expressed in its effects. All psychic phenomena, says Jung, are manifestations of energy, the energy of the process of life; hence the laws governing libido are the laws of vital energy and libido is a quantitative formula for the phenomena of life. It is a dynamic and creative element which streams in outer and inner directions, i.e., towards outer objects and towards the self, ultimately towards the collective unconscious. It can be split, transformed; it can be detached and withdrawn from objects; it can be dammed up; it can regress or be tamed; it can be stored up and canalized; it is what the earlier psychologists called 'will' or 'tendency'; it is desire; it is wish; it is passion; it is interest; it is love; it is the joy of living; it comprises all human activities; it is the foundation and regulator of all psychic existence; it is the driving strength of our own soul; it is cosmic.

As can be gathered from this diversity of definitions, the relation of libido to instinct in the Jungian scheme is rather obscure. In the first place Jung, despite his use of energic terms such as 'damming up' and the like, is plainly averse to describing the energy of libido as a psychic force, indeed maintains that it has nothing to do with the question of the existence of specific psychic force; and in the second he follows the usage of other descriptive psychologists in regarding instinct as an impulsion to certain activities, initiated by outer or inner stimuli which release physical and mental mechanisms. Jung specifically excludes 'will' from the categories of instinct, a view which leads him to the generalization that all psychic activities over which consciousness has no control are instinctive. Now here we begin to get into difficulty. Since, in his view, all psychic processes are (kinetic) energy, and since psychic energy is libido, it follows that instinctual reactions must be libidinal in nature. For example, writing of the 'one-sidedness' of the barbarian, Jung attributes this to his unconscious libido and presupposes that the barbarian suffers from a 'stunting' of his instincts. On the other hand, if, as Jung maintains, libido represents 'will' and if, as he also maintains, 'will' is not instinctual, neither can the libido be instinctual. At another point, however, Jung maintains that the libido has a 'dichotomous way', namely that of instinctual processes in the sense of biological instincts and that of spiritual processes. But since, according to Jung, spiritual processes are psychic, and since instinctual processes, which, again according to Jung, are manifestations of life energy and therefore libidinal, give rise to psychic as well as to somatic processes, and, further, since all psychic activities over which consciousness has no control are instinctive we must conclude that the libido, although instinctual in nature, is nevertheless non-instinctual in nature; which is absurd. Otherwise we must assume that no distinction exists between instinctual and non-instinctual processes (e.g., between instinctual libido and spiritual libido), a view which Jung specifically rejects; or, alternatively, that the libido *ab initio* comprises two entirely distinct orders of energy, in which case the monistic theory of psychic energy is untenable.

Turning for further enlightenment to Jung's account of the phylogenetic vicissitudes of the libido, we find that apparently primal libido was sexual libido. This is implicit in the statement 'Parts of the primal life-force have in course of evolution become de-sexualized', and since the Jungian libido is the primal life-force ' . . . out of which all instincts have been differentiated', it would follow that the sexual instincts are unmodified primal libido, and that all other instincts are phylogenetically sublimated libido. In fact it is Jung's view that in the course of racial development man, turning from one occupation to another, borrowed sexual libido for these purposes and in so doing de-sexualized it; although if, as Jung suggests, *all* human activities are of their nature manifestations of libido, it is not at all clear why it became necessary at some remote period of man's history to de-sexualize libido in order to produce libido which must *a priori* have already existed in a non-sexual state. It would have been all very well for Freud to postulate a phylogenetic sublimation of sexual libido and to attribute the change to some dire events in past history but, having regard to his libido postulates, it is quite inadmissible for Jung to do so. On the other hand, if, as Jung maintains, libido is the driving strength of our soul and if spirit manifests itself in psychic processes or is identical with psychic processes, and if, further, a spiritual process is one of the ways of the libido, and, still further, if libido is either primal sexual energy or de-sexualized psychic energy, it is not at all clear why Jung should reproach Freud on the ground that by his materialistic and biological modes of thought he reduces spirit to 'a mere epiphenomenon produced by a doubtful process of sublimation' (of sexual energies). For if this be a fault, it is a fault of which Jung is himself guilty. Indeed, it is curious to observe that whereas Jung brushes aside the significance of *individual* sublimation established during the infantile development of *modern* man, he is more than ready to postulate an identical process occurring on a grander scale in primitive man at some unspecified epoch and without specified cause.

But let that pass. In the meantime we must note that in Jung's view, although man in some prehistoric time de-sexualized and so differentiated his libido, he persisted in picturing his non-sexual psychic activities in the images of primal sexual libido. Hence the form of the archetypes is usually a sexually symbolic form, although no longer a carrier of sexual libido. Here we are plunged into further confusion as to the nature of the archetypes. Accepting Jung's structural definitions of archetypes as 'organs' af the pre-rational psyche; or as ideas and psychic forms at first without specific content but acquiring content through individual experience of life; or as primordial images; and over-looking the various discrepancies between these definitions and Jung's other view that they are merely inherited thought-dispositions or even reaction-dispositions, we might suppose that archetypes are *activated* by libido, whether modified or de-sexualized. But no: the archetypes, says Jung, are in themselves life forces, protective and healing forces, which, however, if neglected or damaged (*sic*) can set up neurotic and psychotic processes. And since, as he asserts at one point, archetypical ideas can even *spontaneously create themselves*, it would seem that parthenogenetic archetypical energy is inexhaustible. But again no: the inherited arche-typical energy is part of a closed energic system ranging almost effortlessly between consciousness and the Collective Unconscious. 'No psychic value' (i.e., no determining psychic energy) 'can vanish without being replaced by an equiva-

61

lent.' Thus Jung. Here we encounter the penultimate form of his ingrowing theory. 'The idea of energy and its conservation must be a primal image that has slumbered ever (*sic*) in the collective unconscious.' Or, in Jacobi's words, 'The physical law of the conservation of energy and the Platonic notion of the "soul as that which moves itself" are archetypically closely related.' And so we reach the topsy-turvy conclusion that psychic energy is not only a synonym for psychic processes but a 'regulator' of all psychic functions and relations (i.e. processes), both conscious and unconscious.

Although it would be a work of supererogation to speculater as to the motives that led Jung to cleave to a monistic theory of psychic energy, it is scarcely possible to refrain from indicating one of the sources of the confusion in which he lands his ideas. This is a studied refusal to avail himself of metapsychological criteria. Without doubt the adoption of a number of methods of conceptual approach is a tacit admission of the impossibility of describing mental phenomena in one set of terms or analogies. By attempting this hopeless task, Jung discloses his true nature as an academic psychologist, meaning by this designation a psychological observer who cannot think except in terms of consciousness and to whom analysis is merely a descriptive form. The result is a matted confusion, which only a skilled metaphysician could disentangle. Confounding structure with dynamics and dynamics with function, and at the same time seduced by the attractions of facile generalization, of verbal embroidery and of a quasi-scientific mode of expression plentifully besprinkled with archaisms, Jung has developed a sliding-scale of 'meaning' which baffles exactitude. Apparently he cannot, or will not, distinguish between the concept of energy, the sources of energy, the expressions of energy, and the means whereby energy can be regulated. Terms which in Freud's usage had come to acquire specific meaning are flattened out by Jung with the result that his psychology becomes as in pre-Freudian days one-dimensional. Having achieved this by no means inconsiderable

feat, Jung, following the technique of compensation, provides his reader with a complicated system of abstractions
which have lost their anchorage in reality. His concept of
psychic energy comprises everything yet tells us nothing;
or at any rate nothing that a metaphysician speaking from
his armchair could not tell us.

Should there be any doubt on this point it can be readily
dispelled by recourse to empirical criteria. What, we may
ask, is the tendency of this theory; what degree of clinical
understanding do we gain from it; and what price must we
pay for its acceptance? It is well to adopt *clinical* criteria for,
if we leave the matter open to general predilection, we shall
find that concepts of gain and loss depend very largely on
the emotional prejudices of the individual. One can readily
imagine that those who like their psycho-biology neat will
cast their vote for Freud, and that those who like their
psychological pills sugar-coated will plump for Jung whose
gentility of thought is quite impeccable.

In the writer's opinion the tendency of Jung's theories,
and in particular of his theory of psychic energy, is quite
patent. As in the case of the Grand Old Duke of York, who
marched his ten thousand up the hill and down again, the
progress of Jung's theories ever since his defection from
Freud has constituted a Grand Retreat to Conscious Psychology. The psycho-biological pill, being ground down, is
found to consist of nothing but sugar. How could it be otherwise? To re-establish the supremacy of conscious psychology
you must postulate innate instincts or energies or what you
will that do not undergo decisive and permanent modification during individual development; and if perchance you
find unmistakable evidence of important differentiations of
instinct, you must attribute these to phylogenetic influences.
If you find evidence of mental conflict you must assume that
it is due to a clash between phylogenetically determined
forces and purely environment forces. And that is precisely
what Jung does. His monistic *élan vital* wish-washes back
and forward between the archetypes and the conscious life

task. To be sure Jung from time to time attributes to it a catastrophic, almost daemonic, force; but, more often than not, it appears to behave in a remarkably tame manner, at worst to give rise to minor character-difficulties of an intensity that would not ruffle the airs of a suburban drawing-room. In fact, there is little to distinguish the Jungian unconscious libido from the 'sentiments' that are the emotional stock-in-trade of the academic psychologist.

But to reduce the concept of psychic energy once more to this academic status, Jung had first to get rid of the awkward discoveries made by Freud, in particular that the sexual and aggressive energies with which the infant is endowed pass through many primitive phases before they emerge in the highly modified forms that manifest themselves in the private and social life of civilized adults. In Jung's system the whole of infantile sexuality goes by the board. To achieve this end Jung seeks to eliminate the earliest and the latest phases of infantile libidinal development, pointedly ignoring all intermediate stages. The oral libido of Freud he dismisses simply by stating that the 'nutritional phases' of infancy have no sexual component, an *ex-cathedra* opinion which is based apparently on the fact that they do not *seem* to ordinary observation to exhibit sexual features; the excretory phases of infantile libido and the efflorescence of infantile sadism that accompanies them he simply ignores; and the central phase of infantile development, namely, the incestuous (Oedipus) phase he seeks to explain away by means that merit close inspection.

In the first place, although Jung admits that the child may exhibit a kind of rhythmic autoerotism and has a number of habits, e.g., thumb-sucking, which are connected with some phenomena not *non*-sexual, the child's early object relations according to his view, are not to be described as sexual.[1]

[1] It is typical of Jung that although he describes the first of his Stages of Life, i.e. between birth and four years of age, as pre-sexual, he should regard the manifestations of polymorphous infantile sexuality described by Freud as 'preliminary expressions of sexual colouring'

Whatever fixations may take place during very early years are merely a manifestation of babyish egoism. A relatively small number of typical primary patterns are found, all having their origin in early childish experiences. 'The parental complex is therefore nothing but the first manifestation of a clash between Reality and the Individual's Constitutional Inability to meet its requirements.' It *must* be parental simply because parents are the first Reality. The Oedipus complex of Freud although universal is a non-sexual phenomenon indicating at its simplest a desire for possession directed towards the mother by boy and girl alike. Should an erotic element make its appearance, it can be explained as striving to fulfil some archetypical idea. This latter hypothesis is more fully extended in Jung's theory of the neuroses. The adult's failure to meet normal adult demands confessedly does take sexual forms—infantile sexual forms. These are the result of a regression, possibly produced by inability to achieve normal sexuality in adolescence or maturity. Apparently the neurotic regression activates or increases the determining force of certain archetypes but at the same time carries back sexual forms into the state of infantile regression. These sexual manifestations seem to be created by the *later* neurotic personality as part of or symptoms of, the general babyish refusal to break away from the family and 'be one's age.' Actual incest wishes in childhood are, according to Jung, of no more significance than the alleged incest wishes of primitive man; in other words they are of no sexual significance. The infantile incest fantasy is a mythological product, a regressive manifestation due to the revival of archetypes indicating the necessity or desire for rebirth. ' . . . it is most especially the totality of the sun

---

. . . 'it is in this stage that are inaugurated manifestations having so marked a sexual colouring that their relationship is unquestionable although sexuality in the adult sense does not exist'. At the same time he maintains that 'polymorphism' is due to the movement of libido (i.e. Jungian libido, or *élan vital*) 'from the service of nutrition into new avenues', etc. In other words 'sexual colouring' is non-sexual in origin.

65

myth which proves to us that the fundamental basis of the "incestuous" desire does not aim at cohabitation, but at the special thought of becoming a child again, of turning back to the parent's protection, of coming into the mother in order to be born again.' 'But here', says Jung, 'the incest prohibition interferes'; though why an incest barrier enforced by the most ferocious penalties should ever have been necessary to counter these minor sentimentalities is not at all clear. In short, whatever else an incest-wish may be it is not in Jung's view an incest-wish.

In assessing the significance of these, Jung's first gestures of rebellion against the discoveries of Freud one must in fairness recall the darkened emotional atmosphere in which earlier discussions of Freudian theory took place. Now that the facts of infantile sexuality can be and are frequently confirmed by the observations of parents untutored in psychological theory, it is perhaps sufficient to say that if nowadays a budding psychiatrist were to express such sweeping counter-opinions he would be regarded even by most non-Freudian psychologists as a brash ignoramus. No doubt in those early days Jung could not grasp the implications of his own theories. For if infantile sexuality (libido in the Freudian sense) is jettisoned, we are left without adequate explanation of the forces of infantile aggression. Jung is perfectly willing to talk at large and at length of the destructive impulses of the adult, but of infantile sadism and aggression there is hardly a word. One is left to assume that aggression is merely a form of the *élan vital*, possibly but by no means certainly a reactive form. In other words, if we do not postulate, as Freud postulates, aggressive and destructive instincts, we must, according to Jungian principles, regard the phenomena of destruction as part of man's inherited spiritual processes. The whole elaborate history of individual mental development, the phenomena of conscience both conscious and unconscious, in a word, the whole civilizing process undergone by the individual which at its best is responsible for the astounding cultural achievements of man, and at its worst is either unable to stem the uprush of primitive urges or breaks man in the attempt to do so, is reduced to a tussle between constitutional factors and the stresses of current reality, in which the inherited libido plays a neutral role. This, again, is too big a price to pay for the illusory benefits of a comfortable *Weltanschauung*.[1]

And here is perhaps an appropriate point at which to indicate Jung's main, possibly his only claim to consistency of thought. As one wades through his voluminous works, searching amongst a mass of ever-varying definitions for a clear and unqualified statement of Jung's psychological principles one begins to appreciate that despite all the vagueness and inconsistencies of his exposition two tendencies are unmistakable in all his writings—first, a neglect of the developmental achievements of modern man which borders on contempt; and, second, an unswerving determination to produce a psychological system which shall negate at every important point the theories of Freud. Even the neuroses of modern man are regarded by Jung with ill-concealed contempt. To the almost superhuman struggles of the child to effect a compromise between the compelling force of his primitive instincts and the growing harshness of reality, Jung is apparently blind. The neuroses and psychoses of *childhood* which mark the temporary or permanent defeats suffered by the child during these struggles are treated as non-existent. In place of infantile neuroses we are invited to consider the 'problems' occurring during the 'nutritional phase' of life which, according to Jung, extends to the fourth

[1] Space does not permit any detailed account of other sacrifices that would be entailed if Jung's ideas on libido and his absence of ideas on aggression were to be taken seriously. But clearly if the concept of infantile sexuality were to be abandoned and aggression reduced to the level of a phylogenetically modified form of primal libido, we should have to abandon all we have learned regarding the nature of reactive affects, such as morbid anxiety, guilt and depression; and not only the nature of these primitive affects but the decisive part they play in determining human conduct both normal and abnormal; in short their dynamic significance.

year; though even this qualified recognition of *some* form of conflict is contradicted at another point by the sweeping statement that until the age of puberty the child has no problems. The child's main trouble is, it would appear, simply childishness; his main fixations the result of babyish *contretemps*. Small wonder that with this myopic vision Jung, in his search for an explanation of the clamour and conflict of human life, should see only the constitutionally determined inadequacy of adult man to perform his current life-task and ultimately to individuate himself.

Regarding the persistent though not consistent anti-Freudian tendency of Jung's work, it is difficult for a Freudian to speak without drawing to himself the obvious counter that he is a biased critic. It is scarcely a coincidence, however, that Jung, having equated the Freudian unconscious with a system which corresponds mainly with the more superficial Freudian pre-conscious and having in its place erected a Jungian collective unconscious which is in no way derived from individual development, should go on to postulate a form of energy any modification of which must have occurred at an early stage of racial development and to which all human activities are ascribed however fundamentally they may differ. And, although it may seem captious to complain of his selection of terms, it is also not without significance that Jung chose to adapt to his own purposes terms which had already a fixed Freudian connotation. It is easy to understand that the general reader, unfamiliar with the history of these terms and very possibly confusing the Freudian libido with adolescent libidinousness, should form the impression that Jung whilst retaining whatever is of value in Freud has somehow added a new, a spiritual significance to his concepts.

To this vexatious source of confusion we shall have occasion to return when discussing Jung's use of the terms applied by Freud to various unconscious mental mechanisms. For the moment it is more important to indicate the fundamental confusion of thought by means of which Jung seeks to support his studied depreciation of early developmental factors. Generally speaking, Jung's method of dealing with Freudian discoveries is either to ignore them or to proffer alternative hypotheses which cannot be checked by direct clinical observation or experiment and which are as widely displaced from the original Freudian explanations as it is humanly possible to suggest. Fundamental modifications which Freud associated with individual development are displaced to a racial level: psychic energy is also derived from racial levels; it cannot be modified in any important respect by the individual; and to the extent that it can be modified, the essential changes are initiated in conscious layers of the mind. It would seem indeed that Jung has been mesmerized by the concept of phylogenesis and has fallen into the vulgar error of imagining that there is some fundamental difference between phylogenesis and ontogenesis.

To be sure he attempts to safeguard himself by throwing his 'constitutional' net widely, by comprising under the racial factors which model the archetypes of the Collective Unconscious not only the experiences of prehistoric and primitive man but inherited experiences ranging from the biological activities of unicellular organisms down to the ideologies prevalent in the post-Reformation period. 'We need only go back a few hundred years,' he says, 'to reach the conscious level which forms the parallel to our (collective) unconscious content.' So far from safeguarding himself, Jung by this very argument cuts the ground from under his own psychological values. For if the archetypes include elements dating from the Gunpowder Plot we may well question whether the term 'collective' has any specific meaning, or, for the matter of that, why the archetypes should be supposed to be so wise, so venerable and so powerful. Alternatively we may inquire what cosmic influences existed during the Wars of the Roses to modify the libido in such a way that it gave rise to new and inheritable tendencies. In any case Jung seems unable to grasp that the phylogenetically old was once ontogenetically young and in fact crude. Moreover by his own admission

69

the accretions to the collective unconscious are minute; and as he professes that what is inherited is a *tendency* to archaic modes of thinking it is obvious that the products of this tendency must be *repetitive* not cumulative. They cannot improve on themselves: they must, ontogenetically speaking, always be young and crude. From this angle the effect of the Collective Unconscious should be, in the mechanical sense of that term, to 'seize' the whole mental apparatus, not to promote its smooth function.

Such Jungian extravagances may well be due to an inherent reluctance to bridle the pen, a technical qualification not wholly disadvantageous to our popular novelists but certainly a handicap to any scientist. It is perhaps cruel to hold Jung strictly to the letter of his published utterances. But after all one cannot ignore the fact that phylogenesis in its time was ontogenesis. Why should the privilege of ontogenetic development be denied modern man or rather the modern infant? On the other hand why stop at the Reformation? Why not the day before yesterday? Why not here and now? In any case what numinous virtue attaches to phylogenesis? Is it not possible, following the hints given by Jung in his *Modern Man in Search of a Soul*, to attribute Jung's scientific errors to an incurable tendency to apotheosize psychological concepts? At any rate his theories would at once become comprehensible if we were to assume that God is the apotheosis of Phylogeny, of the Archetype, of Energy, of Consciousness and of the Self. But, as we shall see when studying his views on religion and its function, this is an assumption to which Jung will not give his assent, preferring rather to characterize the idea of God as a functional phenomenon or utility appertaining to man.

Strictly speaking, speculations regarding motivation are beyond the scope of a comparative review of psychological systems; although it cannot be denied that Jung himself sets an inviting example in this respect when, commenting on Freud's theory of the neuroses, he says it is no doubt applicable to some cases and indeed that it is best illustrated in the personality of Freud himself. In the present instance speculation over motivations is no doubt also a compensation for, as well as a reaction to, the arduous effort of distilling clear and unequivocal meaning from Jung's work. But it is no substitute for objective appraisal. Be that as it may, we are still under obligation to apply to his system the final test. How does his energy operate? To this crucial point we must now turn our attention.

CHAPTER IV

MENTAL MECHANISMS

A DYNAMIC psychology which cannot indicate the mechanisms whereby psychic energy is distributed through the various mental systems is practically stillborn. Indeed it is almost a contradiction in terms. Yet though the concept of a mental mechanism is the most important of all psychological formulations, it is by far the most difficult to grasp. To do so we must keep constantly in mind the concepts of psychic structure and energy, and in particular those basic postulates regarding mental organization without which it is impossible to build up any psychological system. Of these the most important is Freud's postulate of the *memory trace*. The formulation of this concept is one of the most signal services rendered by Freud to psychological science. The memory trace is the foundation stone of all structural psychology.

It is easy after the event to see that the phenomena of memory held the key to pure psychology. Feeling and conduct could be, indeed often are, explained in ways that call for no postulate of psychic function beyond that of consciousness. But clearly the part played by memory in promoting perceptual correlation and conceptual activity called for a deepening of pre-Freudian one-dimensional psychologies. Freud's postulate of psychic memory traces which can be reactivated when charged with sufficient psychic energy not only provided the necessary groundwork for a new theory of mind but also shattered the aboriginal assumption that mind and consciousness are co-extensive. Consciousness in Freud's view is an *instrument* of an at first undifferentiated psyche taking cognizance of the various stimulations to which it is subject. Obviously, however, an instrument that had to perform simultaneously the functions of perceiving, recording, recalling and correlating psychic stimulations would act at a considerable disadvantage; it would, for example, blur the essential distinction between an actual experience and the memory of it. On the strength of his discovery of 'unconscious' memories, Freud assumed that sensory stimuli coming from without and instinctual excitations coming from within (endopsychic stimuli), in addition to lighting up perceptual-consciousness, pass through this system and produce alterations in the un-differentiated psyche. The burning-in of these records, accelerated by repetition of identical or similar experiences gives rise to the permanent memory trace, which can then be reactivated provided it is charged or recharged with sufficient psychic energy. And psychic energy, it will be remembered, is instinctual energy derived ultimately from somatic sources.

The next step consisted in outlining the development of *systems* of memory traces which with increasing experience of life become more and more elaborate and are finally organized as *ego-structures* both (pre)conscious and uncon-scious. To use modern psycho-analytical terminology, per-ceptual-consciousness is the system round which the ego is built and by means of which ego-structures are established at the periphery of the undifferentiated and non-personal psyche, or, as it is now called, the *Id*.

Now it is characteristic of instinct that it tends to hold to its original aims and objects, and although as the result of internal and external necessity, these aims and objects may be either abandoned or very considerably modified during the course of infantile development, this perseverating ten-dency is not abolished. Instinctual energy tends if frustrated or during states of fatigue to return along the path it origin-ally traced: in other words the charge of psychic energy is withdrawn from more advanced systems of memory traces and retreats to earlier and less complicated systems. As a result of this withdrawal, the earlier aims and objects of the instinct are reactivated. Failing actual gratification, the energy give rise to phantasy-formations. During the state of

73

sleep, for example, the withdrawal of libido from reality is sufficiently extensive to abrogate the function of consciousness and the withdrawn energy gives rise to the complex phantasy formations observed in the dream. This general tendency when organized in the interests of internal or external adaptation is described as the *unconscious mechanism of regression*. It also plays a determining role in mental disorders (maladaptations), in which case a factor of early 'fixation' or partial arrest at an early stage of instinctual development can invariably be discovered. It is sometimes argued that as psychic energy can flow either towards reality or towards the unorganized Id, there is no need to characterize the Id-wards tendency as regressive; but in view of the fact the life proceeds from the intra-uterine to the extra-uterine state, it seems legitimate to describe the backward flow as a regression however recuperative it may be or seem.

In course of development a number of other tendencies of the psychic apparatus are organized and give rise to other unconscious mechanisms. These are classified according to their most characteristic manifestation or effect; but in the long run they vary principally in the way in which they deal with instinctual excitation, i.e., with psychic energy. Thus *repression*, perhaps the best known and least understood of all unconscious mechanisms, succeeds in obliterating all conscious evidence of the existence of any instinctual urge that has fallen under the ban of the super-ego or unconscious conscience. No affective expression or idea exists to give a clue to the forbidden impulse, the energy of which is completely blocked by counter-energies at the disposal of the unconscious ego. In *projection* the outward tendency of an instinctual impulse instead of being recognized as such, gives rise to a feeling that it exists in the minds of other people. In *introjection* and *identification* the ego behaves as if it had unconsciously absorbed or, respectively, adsorbed the characteristics of other people; but in both cases the change is brought about by the necessity to deal with exter-

74

nal frustrations of instinctual energy or to perpetuate within the mind relations with external objects of libidinal importance. Unconscious *displacement* affects both the aim and the objects of instincts; it enables psychic energy to be diverted from the original impulse and distributed freely in an immense number of directions. *Condensation* affects the form of unconscious ideas and permits the expression of two or more impulses in one ideational presentation. *Introversion*, in the Freudian sense, is the result of a withdrawal of libido from external objects giving rise to an efflorescence of phantasy-activity. In what is called *aim-inhibition* the erotic aspects of an original infantile sexual impulse are eliminated, leaving only tender feelings towards the object of the impulse. In *sublimation* the energy of frustrated infantile sexual impulse is desexualized and rendered available for non-sexual aims. And so through the Freudian calendar of unconscious mechanisms.

Although it is impossible to do more than indicate here the general nature of unconscious mechanisms it is essential to the purposes of this review that the reader should bear in mind the following considerations. In the first place although the psychic tendencies that are gradually organized as mental mechanisms are transmitted through the Id and exist from birth, Freud was able to distinguish a hierarchy of mechanisms each one of which plays a determining role at one particular phase of infantile development, and consequently is found operative, either in excess or defect, in mental disorders the fixation point of which lies at any given developmental period. Repression for example, seems to be associated particularly with the mastery of infantile genital libido; and disordered repression is characteristic of both infantile and adult hysterias, the 'fixation' points of which lie at the incestuous phase of development, between the ages usually of three to five years. In the second place *the operation of these mechanisms can be understood only in terms of Freudian theory*, in particular the nature of primary libidinal and aggressive instincts, the existence of the unconscious, pre-conscious and conscious systems of mind, and the development of internal (endopsychic) scrutinising and controlling agencies or unconscious super-ego systems. Whoever rejects Freudian theories and at the same time continues to use Freudian terminology to describe mental mechanisms, must either provide a new and alien meaning for these terms or stand accused of obfuscating his own and his readers' wits.

Bearing these considerations in mind it is comparatively easy to classify Jung's ideas concerning mental economy. A number of these fall into the same category as his libido concept, that is to say, they are expressed in Freudian terms but devoid of Freudian meaning. To this comment the fair-minded reader may react by asking why on earth Jung should not use Freudian terms if he feels they are appropriate to his purpose. He may go on to point out that Freud himself borrowed the term 'introversion' from Jung; although he would be bound to admit that in using this Latinism for 'turning within', Freud was at pains to state precisely in what respects his use of the term differed from that of Jung. Interestingly enough it used to be the habit of writers on the Freud-Jung controversy, Mitchell and Crichton-Miller amongst others, to point out that one of the fundamental differences between Freud and Jung lies in the fact that Jung 'neglects' repression, implying thereby that he does accept the concept but does not think it is so important as Freud made out. This was an unfortunate under-statement. It is quite impossible for Jung to accept the idea of Freudian repression for the reason that having cut loose from Freudian theory, Jung is at sea amongst his own ideas. The process of repression comprises a number of well-defined phases, all of which are concerned with the means whereby derivatives of unconscious impulse (ideas and affects) can be denied expression in the pre-conscious system. Repression, in other words, is concerned primarily with the relations of the (Freudian) unconscious to the (Freudian) pre-conscious system. If you maintain, as Jung does, that Freud's unconscious is for all intents and purposes what Freud would have called the pre-conscious system or alternatively if you describe, as Jung does, a Personal Unconscious that scarcely differs from Freud's pre-conscious, if further you postulate a dynamic Collective Unconscious which is in no way derived from individual development and, still further, if you deny, as Jung does, the existence of an unconscious ego or super-ego, you have surely hamstrung the concept of repression.

If then, from time to time, Jung employs the term repression, it is clear that he cannot mean the repression of Freud. One must therefore scan his writings to see what he does mean. Obviously he is in sore need of some such concept. For one thing he must account for the fact that the core of the Jungian Collective Unconscious remains perpetually unconscious. If, as he says, the forces of the Collective Unconscious are phylogenetic *determining tendencies* which obtain expression in symbols and in various individual idioms that depend on personal experience, he must explain why some of these derivatives secure expression in consciousness and others do not. Still further he must indicate precisely the processes by means of which the repressed material of the Personal Unconscious becomes repressed: and he must indicate equally precisely how conscious derivatives are influenced by these processes. No such explanations are to be found in his writings; on the contrary, a number of specific passages occur indicating that Jung has given his imprimatur to the popular misconception of Freudian repression, namely, that it is a process initiated by the *conscious* system and determined by *conscious* attitudes and sentiments. Thus, indicating the reasons why certain anti-social tendencies are repressed, Jung says: 'Some repress them out of pure cowardice, others on grounds of conventional morality, others again because of regard for their reputation. This repression is either a kind of half-

77

conscious, indecisive letting-go, or a depreciation of the grapes that are out of reach, or again a looking-in-the-other-direction in order not to see one's own wishes.' In other words, *Jung substitutes for Freudian repression the concept of voluntary suppression, one more step, it may be noted, in the direction of an all-inclusive conscious psychology*.

It would be interesting to follow in some detail the implications of Jung's inevitable and, as we have seen, logical abandonment of repression. But to cut a long story short, it follows that by so doing he forfeits the right to use not only the term repression but any other terms for Freudian unconscious mechanisms to which he does not give a new and in principle different meaning. Repression is the keystone of the Freudian system of mental economy and plays a decisive part in maintaining the efficiency of all other (Freudian) unconscious mechanisms. Projection, for example, is a characteristic unconscious mechanism which is distinguished from repression by the fact that both the ideational and the emotional derivatives of instinct do appear in consciousness although in an unrealistic distribution. In the classical instance the individual feels that some other person entertains ideas and feeling-attitudes towards him which really lie in his own mind; and he immediately reacts to these projections with defensive attitudes. But without the auxiliary mechanism of repression, projection would not be able to achieve even this marginal success in dealing with unconscious excitation. Moreover projection, like its companion-mechanism introjection, has a long history. It dates from the time when the unorganized psychic apparatus tends to regard all psychic stimuli as if they came 'from without', passes through a period when the self and the not-self are only partly differentiated, and finally reaches that organized stage when as a fully fledged unconscious mechanism it can act either in the unconscious interests of the ego or to its manifest detriment. But the unconscious ego which projection ultimately serves or injures is the ego as described by Freud; not the ego of Jung, which by his own definition is a conscious system. All therefore that Jung is entitled to say of projection is that it is a *tendency* of the psyche existing from birth.

And significantly enough this is practically all he does say. Indeed it is interesting to note that although Jung intersperses his writings with references to projection, introjection and other Freudian-sounding mechanisms, he seems to be unable to offer more than the vaguest hint as to their mode of operation. In the thirty odd years since he first began to use them for his own purposes, his concepts have not advanced one micro-millimetre. Thus, in his list of definitions introjection signifies a process of 'assimilation', projection of 'dissimilation': introjection is 'an adjustment of the object to the subject', projection 'a discrimination of the object from the subject, by means of a subjective content transveyed into the object'. Generalities of this sort were all very well in their own way and in their own time. But much water has passed under the bridge since they were hailed as daring, provisional hints. The 'subjects' and 'objects' to which they referred were adult subjects and objects. At no point did Jung grasp that the mechanism of introjection is an essential part of a process of ego formation commencing during the later stages of suckling and the early stages of weaning. Under the impetus of Freud's researches the place of Jung's adult subjects and objects is now taken by an elaborate series of cross-sections of the ego and super-ego as they exist during the first five years of the child's life; and by a developmental series of early objects of primitive instincts, the complex vicissitudes of which have been recorded, if not yet fully, at any rate with a considerable wealth of detail. All this was and is a closed book to Jung. Having no child psychology of his own to offer, Jung is compelled to make shift with the formulation of inherited psychic *tendencies* and, by-passing childhood, to make an elaborate play with the superficial complexities of the adult mind.

Nowhere is the rudimentary and retarding nature of

79

Jung's conceptions more apparent than in his description of *introversion*, a mechanism that deserves some attention if only that on it and on the companion mechanism of *extraversion* Jung has founded a type-psychology that has been received with some popular acclaim. The terms 'introvert' and 'extravert' are now bandied about almost as frequently as 'repression' or 'wishful thinking' and with as little understanding of their meaning. Now if we distinguish, as we must, between the *mechamisms* of introversion and extraversion and their *end-results*, e.g., character changes, we find that Jung's account of their operation is limited to a few generalizations of baffling simplicity. Introversion is a 'withdrawing into oneself'; the individual 'sinks into his own depths'. Extraversion on the other hand expresses a fundamental interest in the external world which has therefore an important and essential value for the extravert. Expressed in energic terms introversion represents a centripetal movement of the (Jungian) libido, extraversion a centrifugal movement, resulting, in the one case, in a depreciation of the world and an exaltation of the individual and in the other in reactions of precisely the opposite type. In addition to establishing an *antithetical relationship* between the Jungian Collective Unconscious and the Conscious ('If Consciousness is extraverted, the Unconscious is introverted and conversely'), these movements enable a *compensatory relationship* to be established between the two systems. And this, to all intents and purposes, is all we are vouchsafed regarding the operation of these apparently all-important mechanisms.

Postponing for the moment any examination of the character-psychology based on these simple formulations we may pause to inquire what we actually learn from them regarding the complexities of mental function. The answer is: no more than can be inferred about the activity of mind shortly after birth. As we have seen, Freud's earliest theories regarding primitive mental function postulated movements of instinctual energy from one psychic position to another, the forward flow representing a movement towards discharge (gratification) and the backward flow a regression towards earlier positions. The only difference between these movements and the movements described by Jung as extraversion and introversion is that in the Jungian system extraverted and introverted energies are thought of as moving forth and back between the self and the not-self, between subject and object. Now, from the dynamic point of view, the so-called real world is a collection of objects of instincts, a target for the impulses of the individual and at the same time an obstacle to their gratification; and the so-called retreat from reality is no more than a withdrawal of instinctual energy from its external objects giving rise to a re-distribution of psychic energies within the ego. But whereas Freud was prepared to indicate in any given instance the exact nature of the instinct and the exact nature of the object, and in the case of adults to specify what unconscious infantile mechanisms modify the relation of the adult subject to its objects, Jung by his postulation of a monistic life force (Jungian libido) sacrificed these distinctions in favour of a simple movement of unmodified energy between the adult individual and the world at large. Moreover, by postulating a reciprocal relation between the energies of the Collective Unconscious and those at the disposal of ego-consciousness, not only is modification of energy reduced to a conscious level but *the concept of conflict is reduced to a conscious level*. The libido either meanders gently between one position and another or, should it seek more turbulent expression, has apparently nothing to prevent its discharge save some counter-balancing force directed by Consciousness. In other words, the energy mobilized to balance the extravagances of the *élan vital* is itself *élan vital*. The joy-of-life is held in suspense by the joy-of-life. No wonder the attempt is frequently forlorn and ends in breakdown.

Study of the Jungian concept of introversion provides, however, a convenient starting point for the isolation of purely Jungian ideas of mental dynamics. As we have seen, by abandoning Freud's fundamental theories, Jung deprived himself of the right to use the dynamic concepts employed by Freud. And although the concept of introversion was apparently derived in the first instance from Freudian views as to the flow if instinctual energy, Jung's elaboration of the concept gave some indication of his own theories. These centre round one main assumption, namely, that of the *inevitable complementariness* that governs psychic affairs. 'Energy presupposes necessarily . . . pre-existent antitheses, without which there can be no energy at all. . . . All that lives is energy and is therefore based on antithesis. . . . The process of equalization which is nothing but energy. . . . ' Now according to Jung 'the psyche is a self-regulating system'; hence the problem of opposites is 'a law inherent in human nature'. All mental functions from conscious attitudes and emotions to collective unconscious tendencies, and all interplay between the Conscious and the Collective Unconscious run in consecutive antitheses serving a complementary or compensatory function. And since the total psyche is a closed circuit, rise in energy in one part or system produces a fall in the complementary part or system, sometimes also in the same part or system. Energy is displaceable and can be changed (transformed) by *a direct act of the will* from one opposite to the other. At another point, however, we are told that the change invariably occurs *automatically* when, in the words of Jacobi, 'a fall, a potential difference—psychologically expressed through the pairs of opposites—is present'. Despite being automatic and at the same time subject to conscious acts of will, movement of energy is also *directed* either in progressive or regressive directions. The progressive movement is initiated by consciousness and gives rise to conscious adjustment to the conscious demands of life ; the regressive movement occurs when failure in conscious adjustment brings about a damming up of energy ('obstruction') and so leads to an overcharge of the contents of the Collective Unconscious. Some degree of regression and *a priori* some degree of failure of conscious external adjustment is, however, necessary to bring about internal adjustment, i.e., adjustment to unconscious systems. When this adjustment is achieved, it brings about a restoration of equilibrium and an enrichment of consciousness through the mobilization of health-restoring images and symbols of the Collective Unconscious; these act as 'energy transformers' in consciousness, stem further regression and lead once more to a progressive (conscious adaptive) movement. Should the regressive movement not be stemmed, the Collective Unconscious becomes swollen with *élan vital* and gives rise to neuroses or psychoses. On the other hand a balanced distribution of forces would lead to a 'complete standstill', whatever that is. 'The psychological machine', says Jung, 'that transforms the energy is the symbol'. Apart from temporal movement, energy has *value-intensity*, which is associated with the *image* which in turn is created by phantasy activity out of the material of the Collective Unconscious. This creative phantasy determines the content of meaning which is measured by the *constellation* in which the image appears; so the constellation is also a measure of value-intensity. At another point, however, Jung presents another view. The inner image is a complex factor, 'an integral product with its own autonomous purpose . . . a concentrated expression of the *total psychic situation*, not merely, nor even pre-eminently of unconscious contents pure and simple . . . an expression of the unconscious as well as of the conscious situation of the moment'. Hence its meaning can proceed only from the 'reciprocal relation' of the unconscious and the conscious.

Now if we recall that, accord to Jung, libido itself is the expression of the value-intensity of a psychic process, it is somewhat baffling to find that value-intensity is a second characteristic of the dynamic process which is itself psychic energy or libido. Moreover, if as Jung maintains the movements of libido, whether progressive or regressive, introverted or extraverted, are reciprocal and complementary, and if the conscious and unconscious exist in reciprocal and compensatory relation, not only have we no measure of value-intensity or psychic energy or libido, but the distinction between extraversion and introversion becomes blurred. On the other hand if the reciprocal and compensatory factors are to be taken seriously we must accept equal value-intensities for both conscious and unconscious systems. Why then should the progressive tendency be a purely conscious function? Is not the Collective Unconscious by definition an instigator of progressive movement? Is it not the repository of determining tendencies based on millions of years of phylic experience? And what by the way has happened to the perpetually unconscious core of this Collective Unconscious; what about its general autonomy? The Collective Unconscious, we are told, has, unlike the conscious, a continuity and order independent of us and beyond our influence; the archetypes form its centres and fields of force; they represent an Immediate Psychic Reality which is potentially dangerous to the individual. True, we are also told that the Unconscious is a thing of nature, neutral as far as moral aesthetic and intellectual judgements go, and that it is dangerous only when our conscious attitude to it becomes hopelessly false. It may become explosive owing to repression exercised by 'a cowardly or self-sufficient conscious outlook' (*sic*). In this case surely the false attitude is neither reciprocal nor compensatory but antithetical; and surely if the law of reciprocal influence held good this dangerous potentiality of the Unconscious should create security in the Conscious. Further if energy can be changed by a direct act of will (and 'will', it should be remembered, is according to Jung a non-instinctual manifestation) there seems no reason why any one tendency, whether progressive or regressive, should predominate over its opposite.

But it is as fruitless as it is exasperating to pursue Jung's arguments to their illogical conclusions. It is more to the purpose to eliminate those of his confusions which are due to an apparently inveterate slipshodness of thinking, and to inquire where an acceptance of Jung's general dynamic formulations would lead us. And here the answer is clear enough. It would lead, in the first place, to an absurd over-simplification of mental processes and, in the second, to an exaggeration of the importance of secondary mechanisms; it would lead to a neglect of primary psychic forces and to a scaling-down of conflict to a conscious level; it would ignore those truly staggering achievements in the way of instinct-modification which are compassed during the childhood of the individual; and it would put out of court the concepts of defence mechanisms and of instinctual barriers which serve to distinguish unconscious from preconscious function. It is not enough to say, as Jung does, that all human activities are psychic energy, to call this energy libido, and to add that this energy flows in various directions. It is certainly absurd to magnify the secondary mechanisms of compensation to the proportions of an inherent tendency governing all psychic relations. It is equally absurd to advance an automatic system of antithetical relations to explain away phenomena that are due in the last analysis to the existence of unconscious conflict. And it is standing dynamic psychology on its head to say that conscious tendencies and end-products have the same 'value intensity' as primary unconscious mechanisms and forces. For if, as even Jung is ready at times to admit, the behaviour of man represents in the long run a compromise between his inner tendencies and the conditions imposed on him by outer reality, we cannot at the same time maintain that a compromise has the same driving or directing force as the opposing elements which give rise to it. Observing Jung's dogged attempts to maintain this dynamic contradiction, one can well understand why he was at pains to postulate a monistic psychic energy and to confine it within a closed circuit. For in the final analysis his dynamic psychology boils down to the statements that psychic activity is energy, that energy is energic in nature and that it regulates itself.

And here perhaps it is convenient to summarize the conclusions arrived at from a survey of Jung's general theory of mind and at the same time to indicate its general relation to Freudian theory. To state the case as briefly as possible: *there is no evidence that Jung has grasped the nature of unconscious processes; his claim to be a dynamic psychologist is extremely weak, certainly no stronger than that of any 'conscious' or 'academic psychologist'*; indeed *his whole system is based on conscious and descriptive criteria.* In other words *the key to the riddle of Jung's psychology is that Jung is a conscious psychologist.* As for the relation of his psychology to Freudian psychology all that need be said is that it has little or no relation to Freudian psychology: *The mostly implicit but often explicit tendency of his theories is to prove that Freud's discovery of the unconscious and of the laws that regulate its functions is either inaccurate, totally false or totally unnecessary.* Whether he knows it or not, this is Jung's consuming passion.

To the enthusiastic anti-Freudian this last conclusion may suggest a much to be desired consummation: but to the un-oriented reader anxious, like most natural eclectics, to be fair and at the same time to extract the best from both schools, it may not be clear why the irreconcilable differences existing between the psychology of Freud and that of Jung are of such consequence. To clarify the position let us assume for argument's sake that Jung's theories are valid. What follows? The Unconscious of Freud disappears to give place to an unpredictable constitutional factor (the so-called Collective Unconscious and its Archetypes). Let us be clear about this. The Personal Unconscious of Jung has not the remotest resemblance to Freud's unconscious system. And no scanty lip-service to repression can retrieve the situation. Repression is incompatible with the Jungian system. Jung in fact never got nearer to the Freudian unconscious than Janet, whose phenomenological description of a 'subconscious' together with his concepts of 'psychic tension' and 'molar dissociation'[1] would amply cover Jung's theoretical requirements. There is no way out of the impasse. If Jung is right the unconscious must go and with it must go repression. The barriers between the unconscious and the conscious being thus thrown down, the concept of unconscious conflict must also disappear. Consciousness regains its pristine pre-Freudian status as the totality of mind. 'Mind' in any case is considered by Jung as an intellectual function.

But this is not all. A reaffirmation of the overriding executive functions of consciousness and a return to the old, academic, one-dimensional view of mind makes it necessary to flatten out any vital distinction between the varieties and sources of psychic energy. And so at one fell swoop the painfully acquired distinction of fundmental instincts and of the modifications they undergo is obliterated. Infantile sexuality must go. Sexuality regains its pre-Freudian adult connotation. And with infantile sexuality and its complicated account of family love and hate goes the 'transference', a special variety of unconscious displacement from infantile life to the 'therapeutic situation' which first afforded us insight into the nature of psycho-therapy. Instead we must operate with a concept of *élan vital* which forbids us to make any fundamental distinction between

---

[1] Studying the phenomena of *hysteria*, Janet concluded that consciousness could be split into two or more currents, the *dissociated* current being neither perceived nor controlled by the main stream of consciousness. This involved, in his view, the existence of a (phenomenological) *sub-conscious*. Turning to the investigation of other, non-hysterical, neuroses which he included under the general heading of *psychasthenia*, Janet maintained that these are due to a failure of normal integration of mental processes. In this case the dissociation is *molecular* whereas in hysteria it is *molar*. Both molecular and molar dissociation are due in Janet's opinion to a lowering of that niveau of *psychological tension* which in normal persons produces effective integration. *The psychic processes taking place in Janet's sub-conscious have however all the characteristics of normal conscious processes save that of integration with the main stream.* Janet's sub-conscious is thus a concept entirely distinct from the Freudian concept of a dynamically unconscious system.

psychic activities. Finally, if anything further were needed to oppose the Freudian concept of unconscious conflict, it would be the Jungian concept of a closed psychic system regulated by a series of automatic laws of opposites and compensations.

The unconscious, infantile sexuality, repression, conflict and transference: these, said T. W. Mitchell, one of the wisest and fairest minded of British psychologists, 'seem to me to be the fundamental conceptions of psycho-analysis and anyone who accepts them may be said to accept psycho-analytic teaching'. And these are precisely the conceptions that must be abandoned if we are to accept Jung's teaching. With them we must abandon also the unconscious ego, unconscious conscience and the foundations of character. We must, in short, abandon child psychology. We must forget that the child is the father of the man and remember instead that the Collective Unconscious is the father and mother of Adult Man who apparently springs on to the stage of life full-witted and with a quiver-full of automatic and inherited mechanisms ready at hand.

CHAPTER V

CHARACTER AND CONSCIOUSNESS

HOWEVER fascinating the story of man's mental development may be, it is scarcely fair to expect the general reader to enjoy, even if he can always follow, the complexities of unconscious mental function. And so far we have been concerned for the most part with the general theories of unconscious mental function advanced respectively by Freud and by Jung. The situation is aggravated when as in the present instance the account has been compressed to the smallest space compatible with intelligibility. In any case the reader might well complain of both psycho-analysts and 'analytical psychologists', to use the description of themselves officially adopted by Jungians, that, being immersed in the anatomy and physiology of mind, they frequently appear to lose sight of its total function; or at any rate that they frequently omit to build up from their microscopic studies a recognizable portrait of man. A good deal of the hostility with which psychological essays are greeted is due to the fear men experience when they cannot recognize themselves.

Nor is the criticism entirely unfounded. Of the many myths that have grown round the modern equivalent of the medicine man, two are particularly tenacious of life. It is commonly believed that a psychologist can read the minds of those with whom he comes even in casual contact; and he is generally held to be a shrewd judge of character. Nothing could be further from the truth. Deprived of his instruments of investigation, the professional psychologist is left wondering what goes on in other people's minds; and his assessments of character are much less shrewd than those of the average commercial traveller. As a matter of interest the myth that Hitler was possessed of uncanny psychological insight was merely a popular and super-

stitious exaggeration of his actual abilities as an unscrupu-
lous salesman. Defining character in the first instance as the
integrated sum of the individual's behaviouristic and emotional patterns and potentialities, we may safely say that a
professional psychologist's judgement of character is no
better than that of the average man and much poorer than
that of the average novelist.

There is, however, an obvious deduction to be drawn
from this state of affairs. Indeed it is only fair to the clinical
psychologist to say that his pedestrian judgement in everyday matters is due in part to his constant pre-occupation
with unconscious mechanisms and motivations. Rightly
convinced of the importance of these determinants of
human conduct, he gives them pride of place. By so doing
he neglects the fact that character, which is essentially the
active organized cortex of the psyche, is a precipitate of
compromises effected between the unconscious mind and
its environmental influences. Again as a matter of interest
the clinical psychologist's shrewdest judgements are made
either when the character of his subject corresponds most
closely to some abnormal pattern or symptom; for example,
when a 'ritualistic type' of individual behaves in his everyday life in a way that is reminiscent of the clinical symptoms of a true obsessional neurosis; or when, flanked by
batteries of clinical 'tests' both ancient and modern, he
exercises the professional privilege of betting on a virtual
certainty after making an exhaustive clinical examination.
Of clinical case histories it can only be said that, except in
the rarest of instances, they are classroom diagrams rather
than portraits. The psycho-analyst, as has been said, is a
craftsman, not an artist.

On the other hand, the existence of this very difficulty
provides us with a practical test of any given psychological
system. We can always inquire how much light it throws on
the processes of character formation, and whether it can
provide a useful classification of character 'types'. For purposes of definition we may say that a useful classification is

one which avoids undue elaboration without being so simplified as to include under any one heading types that cry out for differentiation.

This second condition is a stumbling block to most 'type' classifications. While, for example, it is fundamentally sound to say that mental activity is expressed in ideas, in affects (feelings, emotions) and in behaviour (voluntary or involuntary), a broad classification of intellectual types, emotional types and action types is no sooner launched than it founders from sheer topheaviness. It is misleading into the bargain. For as we know, often to our cost, the intellectual type may be frankly 'stupid' or reasonably 'wise', he may be emotionally sensitive or emotionally impoverished; he may be reckless or over-restrained in action. Moreover, classifications of this kind give little or no indication of the underlying character on which accurate prognostications of conduct ultimately depend. For our interest in character is primarily aroused by our instincts of self-preservation and by the overriding need to avoid frustration. Our main concern is to know at first sight whether a person is likely to behave towards us in a friendly or unfriendly manner, to gratify or frustrate our impulses. Here therefore are two sound tests of a character classification; first, whether it enables us to make reasonably accurate prognostications and, second, whether it indicates the 'effective' character as apart from the standard 'façade' of character which the individual, often in all conscious sincerity and with the best of conscious motives, turns towards us. Our intellectual, for example, may on occasions of real crisis behave like a child, the childish hysterical type may on similar occasions behave with sound adult commonsense, provided of course the occasion does not touch him on some neurotic tender spot. A character classification should therefore indicate how much of the potential child lies behind the adult personality. In short, since one of the arts of character is to conceal character, a good classification should function as a key as well as a card index.

When we come to compare the Jungian system of characterology with that developed along Freudian lines, certain outstanding differences come to light. In the first place Freud was never at pains to make characterological differentiations a central part of his clinical formulations. True his writings are freely interspersed with vivid thumb-nail sketches of individual character types; and he repeatedly outlined the fundamental laws that govern character formation. But systematic work on this subject was contributed for the most part by Freud's immediate followers. And in the first instance it took the form of descriptions of these character formations which could be correlated with infantile phases in the *development of the libido*. Hence the terms oral, anal and genital character, indicating respectively the imprint on ego-structure and reaction of the child's passage through the sucking, the excretory and the genital phases of infantile life. These were subsequently subdivided in accordance with whether the character formation indicated the influence of *gratification* or *frustration* of instinct respectively. Thus a gratified oral type tends to be optimistic and generous, a frustrated oral type impatient, envious, grudging and easily depressed; a gratified anal type amenable, capable of generosity of a rather conditioned type, punctual and punctilious and on the whole given to order and pedantry; a frustrated anal type grudging, parsimonious, mean, negativistic and either excessively untidy or ritualistic to the point of absurdity. In view of Jung's main division of humanity into extraverts and introverts it is interesting to note that both oral and anal gratified types have comparatively easy contacts with the external world whereas the frustrated types are inturned and absorbed in their bodily and mental functions. And we may suspect that broad groupings such as that of extraversion and introversion actually obstruct more than they advance the classification of character traits. Naturally there are other possible sub-divisions of the main *instinctual character groups*. For example, they can be divided into *positive* or

92

negative types in accordance with the tendency to give expression to or to oppose early instinctual drives. This is clear in the case of the tidy ritualists and these ritualists who express themselves in constant untidiness.

But obviously these *character components*, whether positive or negative, frustrated or gratified, do not represent the *total* libidinal character. However scattered his early sexual components may be, man is essentially a bisexual animal; and some of the main outlines of his character depend on how he weathers the infantile phase of homosexuality and how far he achieves a successful heterosexual genital interest. One of the truly gigantic tasks facing the psycho-analyst is the classification of unconscious homosexual types, which, incidentally, must be clearly distinguished from persons whose sexual organization is manifestly inverted. There are, of course, many larval inverts who, though heterosexual in practice, manifest obvious physical and mental stigmata of homosexuality. But the true unconscious homosexual is not so easily defined. Some can, however, be readily distinguished at the cocktail bar, where gin-drinking and often elegant women of a brittle and easily depressed disposition enjoy the luxury of being 'a man amongst men' whose character closely approximates to their own, and with whom they enjoy rather promiscuous relations of a studiedly sophisticated but usually unsatisfying nature.

To add to these complications, the libidinal character is influenced at every stage of its development by patterns of reaction developed by the individual to deal with his *unconscious aggression*, in particular the sadistic and masochistic components derived from a fusion of his libidinal and destructive instincts. The most important estimates of instinctual character depend on the way in which libidinal and aggressive tendencies combine. Obviously expansive friendly types can be contrasted with reserved or negativistic types, dominating and aggressive sadistic types with diffident and self-sacrificing masochistic characters. But the

93

most significant sub-group is that in which ambivalence of feeling and attitude is expressed, giving rise to such varied reactions as doubt, indecision, inertia, fickleness, inconsistency, also to a number of 'paired' reactions such as alternating hyper-sensitiveness and callousness towards external objects.

Next in order of importance comes the isolation of character-patterns due to the operation of one or more *unconscious mechanism*. One of the earliest observations in this direction concerned the influence of the unconscious mechanism of projection, by means of which painful psychic excitations are treated as if they originated without the personality and are then reacted to as objectionable or dangerous. The projective character-type may exercise his disgruntled hypersensitivity at any point in his familial and social contacts, is a notoriously difficult marriage partner, and, when he takes to politics, an insensate reformer. Following this line of approach the influence of minor faults in or exaggerations of the mechanism of repression was held to account for such reactions as absent-mindedness, unreliability, rigidity of thought, perturbation over trivial occasions and the like. But above all the mechanism of reaction-formation, whereby unconscious impulses are held in check by ideas and attitudes of an antithetical nature, proved to be the mainstay of character-formation. The over-solicitous type, quick to pity, roused to indignation at the idea of injury to animals, diffident in contact and argument but nevertheless opinionative and emotionally aggrandizing, rather oppressively self-sacrificing yet not a little of a tyrant, provides in caricature an illustration of the reaction-formation type. Naturally there are as many types of reactive-character as there are components of instinct.

Classification of character-formations in terms of their instinctual source or dynamic function soon led to the study of those unconscious mechanisms which produce a direct and lasting imprint on the *structure of the ego*. Two examples must suffice: first, those unconscious identifications, either friendly or hostile, with family figures which leave a permanent imprint on the character of the child and may largely determine his adult conduct; and, second, those more profound absorptions of parental influences (introjections) that go to build up the unconscious conscience. Here surely is a key to many of the riddles of character-formation; and here we can pigeon-hole the imitative types, the histrionically masculine woman or feminine man, the mother-fixated son and father-fixated daughter, the revolutionary and the conservative, the leader and the follower, the guilt-ridden apologists for their own existence, and the hard-bitten egoists whose callousness or lack of sympathy borders often on a pathological anti-social disposition.

From this approach it is a short step to the correlation of character groups with *classical forms of mental disorder*. This, perhaps the most useful of all classifications, certainly that which allows a maximum accuracy in prognostication, is based on the fact that whereas, for example, the neurotic *isolates* his symptoms from the rest of the ego, often encapsulates them, the normal person perpetually discharges his lesser conflicts *through his personality*, thereby producing typical character-formations. So far we have no exact statistical evidence to go on, but it is not far short of the mark to say that the human race can be divided up into hysterical, obsessional, depressive, alcoholic, hypochondriacal, paranoid, schizoid and psychopathic[1] *types*, meaning thereby that they exploit in their individual and social relations unconscious mechanisms which if more exaggerated would give rise to classical neurotic, psychotic or psychopathic symptoms. The anxious but histrionic woman whose life is an endless ring of fitful emotional episodes and crises, mainly self-induced; the emotionally inhibited

[1] The true psychopath is neither neurotic nor psychotic, but exhibits a general instability of emotion, thought and conduct, is frequently sexually perverted and often anti-social: in fact the psychopath was formerly described as a 'moral imbecile'.

pedant who regulates his life with rigid obsessional systems and time tables; the wretchedly inferior and guilt-ridden individual silently clamouring for love but provoking rejection; the hail-fellow-well-met who cements life-long friendships at the local pub only to find that they have disintegrated by closing time; the secret drinker who is never drunk; the valetudinarian preoccupied with the metaphysics of intestinal function; the theosophical-minded vegetarian who stocks his lavatory shelves with the literature of uplift; the world-reformer turning a corrosive eye to the shortcomings of modern civilization for which he has in pickle a sure-fire system of redemption; the inturned and impenetrable narcissist so concerned with the discovery of God in his own unconscious ego that he lives in a social vacuum; the scatterbrained but often highly intelligent ne'er-do-well causing friction and injury wherever he goes up to the point when he has passed the male change of life; all these are exaggerations of types that can be recognized anywhere and whose conduct in a crisis can be almost unfailingly prognosticated.

To these formal and classified groups can be added a Theophrastian collection of 'special types' isolated on the strength of some characteristic or outstanding pattern of behaviour. Literature abounds in examples of this mainly descriptive group: the miser, the gambler, the misanthrope, the misogynist, the prig, the bully, the moaner, the improvident, the hypocrite, the croaker, the optimist, the scapegoat, the seducer, the gold-digger, the braggart and the egoist. And it must be admitted that the task of description has been infinitely better done by the realistic novelist than by the professional psycho-analyst, whose main qualification to write on the subject is a technical understanding of underlying mechanisms. Nevertheless, the psycho-analyst has added many special types to the list, as witness Freud's clinical descriptions and analyses of the 'criminal impelled by unconscious guilt', the 'family-fixated romantic', 'the unconscious victim of success', not to mention innumerable other analytical etchings of dominating character reactions. Indeed we may anticipate with some confidence not unmixed with dismay the carrying out of an increasing number of psycho-analytical post-mortems on the great figures of history and fiction. Already the psychological anatomy of Hamlet, Lear, and other Shakespearian figures has been displayed on psycho-analytical diagrams and it will not be long before we are regaled with an account of the mainsprings of the character of Alceste, Mr Earlforward, Falstaff, Père Goriot, Sir Charles Grandison, Mrs. Gummidge, Tom Jones, Moll Flanders, Lovelace, Mr. Micawber, Col. Newcome, Aunt Norris, Mr Oldbuck, Sir Willoughby Patterne, Mr. Pecksniff, Mrs. Proudie, Don Quixote, Becky Sharp, Thersites, my Uncle Toby—and all. Depressing as the prospect may be to the student of history or literature, the psycho-analyst cannot and in any case will not be denied the right to ransack both fields for confirmation of his views regarding the mainsprings of human conduct. All that we may require of him is that he should refrain from aping the manners and preciosities of the *litterateur* and that he should not pretend to an esoteric sagacity and infallibility he in no wise possesses.

The foregoing account of Freudian characterology has been presented in some detail for two reasons. In the first place it gives a better idea of the scope and methodology of psycho-analysis than can be gathered from a detailed account of psycho-analytical theory, which, at the best of times, is apt to lose its outline in a maze of technicalities. And in the second place it affords us some criteria with which to evaluate the type-psychology of Jung. To which may be added that characterology deals with a variety of clinical material accessible to every layman, who may therefore legitimately claim to have an opinion of his own as to the value of any particular system.

An opinion, yes; but alas! not the last word. For the existence of unconscious factors in character-formation renders it
necessary to keep constantly in mind the theoretical basis of
any characterological system. Jung, for example, sets out on
his character studies armed with the concept of *autonomous
complexes*, by which he means emotionally toned contents
having a certain amount of unconscious autonomy and offer-
ing resistance to conscious intentions. These, he thinks, may
be either obstacles or stimuli to new possibilities of achievement. Primary patterns of this sort exist in relatively small
numbers, but the ways in which the complex works itself
out are infinitely varied. By this means individual dispositions
are recognized. And starting with a contrast between
reflecting and unreflecting types, Jung went on to describe
types of individual who when reacting to a given situation
'draw back a little as if with an unvoiced "No",' and
'another class who in the same situation come forward with
an immediate reaction'. The former corresponds to the *introverted*, the latter to the *extraverted type*. Both represent 'an
essential bias' determining behaviour and subjective experience and 'denoting the compensatory activity of the
unconscious which we may expect to find'.

The Jungian mechanisms responsible for these subjective
and objective 'attitude-types' and the laws of compensation
that govern their relation to the Collective Unconscious and
to consciousness have been indicated in the previous chapter.
It remains to add that both introversion and extraversion are
held to be biologically determined and can be altered during
individual development only under very special circumstances, which are chiefly biological in nature, e.g., at
puberty or the climacteric (change of life). The introverted
unconscious of the extravert is undifferentiated, impulsive
or compulsive ; hence when it breaks through and clashes
with the extraverted conscious, it is immediately projected
on to introverted objects. The break-through of unconscious
extraversion in an introvert makes him an inferior, un-
adjusted extravert. When a situation arises which the extra-
98

vert cannot deal with, the opposite 'habitus' tries to deal with it; but, being unconscious and neglected, generally makes a mess of it. This failure may be the first sign of the individual's natural type. Conflicts of this kind are said to happen mostly in the second half of life. Generally the extravert gets on better in the first half of life since adjustment to external circumstances is more important at that stage. The introvert gets on better in the second half. Apparently to avoid confusion, extraverts and introverts are labelled according to the *conscious* attitude. On the other hand, every individual, we are told, possesses both mechanisms, and only relative predominance of one or other determines the type, indicating presumably that the conscious balance sets the type which then by the law of compensation sets the unconscious type, which can, however, upset the conscious type if the conscious type is upset by reality.

But to turn from theory and dynamics to the collection of distinctive traits of character (end-products), Jung's general extraverted type may be described as an individual whose interest is primarily directed outwards; objective; full of self-expression and self-confidence; looking for himself in other people; flourishing in the regard of others and, in the non-sexual sense of the term, exhibitionistic; turning events to his own purposes; acting on first impressions and thoughts; and, on the whole, gregarious. By contrast the introverted type turns his interest inwards; is subjective; inhibited in self-expression and therefore lacking in self-confidence; detached in attitude and seemingly indifferent to the concerns of others; walking like the cat alone; making heavy weather of external responsibilities; acting chiefly on reflection or at any rate on second thoughts; and if not fundamentally solitary, at least on the defence against external circumstances.

No sooner had Jung effected these main sub-divisions of human character than he found himself dissatisfied. 'I discovered to my dismay that somehow or other I had been taken in by it' (his classification) . . . 'I had tried too much and in too simple a way . . . an introvert does not simply draw back and hesitate before the object, but . . . does so in a very definite way.' Seeking a fresh approach, Jung fell back on a system which bears a close resemblance to the old 'faculty psychology' but which, he assures us, is based on standards accepted of the people. In so doing he gave a clearer outline to his anatomy of consciousness. Consciousness can be mapped out in terms of psychic *functions*; namely, thinking, feeling, intuition, and sensation. Incidentally this distinction of *functional types* cleared up the confusion caused by Jung's earlier identification of introverted with thinking types and of extraverted with feeling types. This, he confesses, was a mistake. The introvert may or may not be a thinking type, but if he is he thinks in the interests of introversion, and so, *mutatis mutandis*, with extraversion and feeling.

Two further points: sensation and intuition are in Jung's view non-rational functions, whereas both thinking and feeling subserve rationality, since feeling too is used in valuation; secondly, a hierarchy of functions exists varying for different types. The most exercised constitutes the *superior* function to which a second and sometimes a third function can act as major and/or minor accessories. The fourth or inferior function being unexercised remains in a primitive or infantile state 'often only half-conscious or even quite unconscious'. It constitutes a specific inferiority, is beyond our control and may victimize us. Here the term 'unconscious' is used in both descriptive and dynamic senses for, as we have seen earlier, neglected functions sink also into the Collective Unconscious. These four functions constitute Jung's four cardinal points, 'arbitrary and indispensable', implying thereby that each function has a polar opposite; sensation is opposed to intuition and feeling to thought. Like attitude types, function types are constitutionally determined; they are hereditary characteristics or tendencies.

Multiplying the functional types by the attitudinal types,

we have thus eight main variations: (1) the introverted thinker; more interested in concepts than facts, a theoretician, dogmatic and intellectually arrogant, lacking in feeling and intuition, devoid of sensation but sensitive to criticism; (2) the extraverted thinker: a worshipper of facts from which he loves to build theories, intolerant, fanatical and given to proselytizing; (3) the feeling introvert; a feminine type, adapting by feeling valuations, reacting with strong likes and dislikes which, however, he is incapable of expressing, tactless and incompetent in personal relations and much misunderstood; (4) the feeling extravert; also a feminine type, ready to identify with others particularly on a conventional basis, tending to exhaust the emotions in external relations, readily suggestible and quick to overvalue, inhibited in thinking capacity; (5) the sensorial introvert; irrational and incalculable, reacting through subjective sensation, a sensualist who projects his unconscious fears on to the world which he senses archetypically; (6) the sensorial extravert; hungry for external stimuli which must, however, be rapidly changed, easily bored and impatient, well meaning but inconsiderate and either sensorial or refined in his external values; (7) the intuitive introvert; primarily subjective with little concern for external circumstances, unstable and undependable in relations, reading the world in terms of his own Collective Unconscious, obtuse in understanding and easily misunderstood; (8) the intuitive extravert; also unstable and changeable, seemingly optimistic, impulsive and positive, subject to error in long-distance relationships but a good man in an emergency. These eight groups are further subdivided in accordance with the existence of ancillary or 'co-functions' which, however, are never the polar opposite of the superior function. And since this secondary function may belong to the opposite attitudinal group from that of the superior function, e.g., a sensorial introvert may have a co-function of extraverted thinking, the ultimate number of character variables is very great indeed.

101

When attempting to evaluate Jung's characterological system, it is essential to remember that it is based on a descriptive study of conscious *end-products*. There is all the difference in the world between his *primary mechanisms* of extraversion and introversion and the extraverted and introverted *character traits* he describes. The view that Jung's attitudinal types represent a *fundamental* character antithesis based on the operation of two fundamental mechanisms will not bear a moment's examination. As we have seen, qualitative differences in character formation can be traced to different components of the (Freudian) libido. A gratified oral and anal type exhibits many of the characteristics that Jung would call extraverted, a frustrated or negative oral type is a Jungian introvert *par excellence*. An (unconsciously) homosexual character is less extraverted than a heterosexual genital type. A positive aggressive type is apparently extraverted yet may be exquisitely narcissistic, i.e., introverted in the Jungian sense. A negative aggressive type may appear to be introverted to the point of complete inhibition, yet he may be defending himself against a tendency to aggressive extraversion so violent that it paralyses all his relations to objects. In short the vicissitudes of object relations and of the instincts directed towards objects, give rise to an infinite variety of character reactions which, when shoe-horned into the descriptive categories of extraversion and introversion, lose thereby whatever *specific* characteristics they may possess.

It is unnecessary to labour this argument at much length. It will scarcely be denied that a schizophrenic manifests extreme forms of introversion: yet there are times when it is impossible to distinguish a schizophrenic from a true hysteric who could legitimately be described as a frightened, disappointed and angry extravert. And a like confusion arises in the case of hysterical and melancholiac depression respectively. An individual given to projection is certainly an extravert as regards his aggression but only rarely as regards his love impulses which are as a rule thoroughly

102

introverted. There must be few Lotharios who have not had their faces slapped because of a failure to recognize the difference between an unconsciously homosexual and a heterosexual extravert: just as there must be few who in their expectant approaches to apparently shy introverts have not at times been pleasantly surprised by flushing a covey of true extravert reactions. An introverted son by identifying with an extravert mother can deny his nature both as a male and an introvert. Likewise a 'naturally' extraverted daughter can deceive herself and her neighbours through an identification with a 'naturally' introverted father. The fact is that descriptive labels such as introversion or extraversion cannot give the remotest hint of the elaborate and complicated dynamic and structural developments that give rise to these end-results. Consequently they are useless for the purpose either of discrimination or of prognostication.

The fair-minded reader, his sympathies generously aroused by apparently unsparing criticism, may well inquire, 'Why labour the point? Didn't Jung himself admit that his first classification was over-simple?' To be sure he did: but as is so often the case with Jung's candid admissions, the retreat is made *pour mieux sauter*. Having made the cardinal blunder of confusing conscious end-products with two out of many primary tendencies inherent in libido (whether Jungian or Freudian), Jung proceeded unabashed to rectify this blunder by multiplying it by four. By subdividing his main character types in terms of *four functions*, namely, thinking, feeling, intuition and sensation, Jung not only irrevocably saddled this characterology with conscious and descriptive criteria, but arbitrarily cut through the developmental phases, during which these functions are inextricably dovetailed, to postulate basic constitutional and therefore inherited tendencies. Between the conscious end-product and the constitutional tendency a yawning gap exists, which Jung either refuses to fill or is incapable of filling.

To this round criticism the reply may no doubt be made that Jung does *not* neglect developmental factors and that his functional criteria are *not* wholly conscious. It is true, for example, that he regards intuition as a transmission of perceptions 'in an unconscious way': subjective intuition is, he says 'a perception of unconscious psychic facts whose origin is essentially subjective'; objective intuition 'a perception of facts which depend on subliminal perceptions of the object and *upon the thoughts and feelings occasioned thereby*'. (Author's italics.) 'Intuition', Jung adds, 'is a characteristic of infantile and primitive psychology'. Moreover, being unconscious it is an irrational function. But despite the use of the term 'subliminal', which might suggest the action of the Personal Unconscious, it is clear from the various contexts that this unconscious element is derived from the Collective Unconscious to which indeed inferior intuition, we are informed, necessarily returns, there to perform a compensatory function. The long and tortuous history of individual development of (in the Freudian sense) unconscious cognitive processes, the systems of control and at the same time the infinite elaboration of conceptual processes contributed by the deeper layers of the (Freudian) pre-conscious, and with them the whole history of infantile development of reality sense, are totally ignored. We are left with a definition that would place the paranoid lunatic with his delusions of persecution in the same category as the man with a hunch.

It is also true that, in a sentence which deserves full quotation, Jung cuts the ground from under his fourfold *basic* distinctions. Writing of sensation he describes it as 'a prominent characteristic *both in the child and the primitive* in so far as it *always predominates over thinking and feeling*, though not necessarily over intuition. For I regard sensation as conscious, and intuition as unconscious perception. For me sensation and intuition represent a pair of opposites, or two mutually compensating functions, like thinking and feeling. Thinking and feeling as independent functions are

104

developed both ontogenetically and phylogenetically from sensation and equally, of course, from intuition as the necessary counterpart of sensation.' (Author's italics throughout.) A like admission is made when, classifying thinking as a *basic* apperceptive activity, he goes on to differentiate *active* and passive thought-activity and calls passive thinking *intuitive* thinking. If thinking can be intuitive why make a basic distinction between intuition and thinking?

In any case, it is not possible to have it both ways. It requires no very detailed study of auditory-, visual- and olfactory- (smell) thinking to grasp that conceptual processes must have developed through the correlation of memory traces of perceptual experiences and that they must vary in function accord according to whether they are used in the interests of reality adaptation, or of phantasy gratification. It is equally easy to see that originally thinking must have been of the concrete 'thing type' as distinct from the more abstract 'word type', and that at all stages of its development it must have been influenced by affective (emotional) experiences and by the 'principles' or laws of psychic function which pleasure-pain experiences set in motion. It is not hard to see that intuition depends on the operation of unconscious as distinct from pre-conscious mechanisms, and that its accuracy depends on whether the mechanisms are used in the interests of unconscious (subjective) phantasy or of reality adaptation. We may even speculate with Freud whether the unconscious system has still other modes of communication with external objects which operate without the interference of the pre-conscious or the interposition of consciousness. But if we adopt this developmental approach and concede the overwhelming importance of infantile phases *common to all persons* during which all functions act in close concert but manifesting an increasing tendency towards conceptual thinking, we cannot possible accept a classification which divides humanity in terms of four basic functions constitutionally inherited and incapable except in the rarest conditions of voluntary modification, yet at the

105

same time retroactive, polar, compensatory and subject to acts of will.

The truth is that Jung's cursory references to the developmental aspects of his 'functions' may be taken at their face value, which is practically nil. His whole discussion of character is expressed in that metaphysical idiom once the common property of the academic psychologist and of the theologian. Despite the apparently endless permutations and combinations arising from his two-, four- and eightfold categories, human character is seen by the Jungian as a thing of circles, quadrants, compass points and polarities. And despite a good deal of play with the concepts of energy and adaptation, his character types are essentially static. Character is like a piece of cake to be divided into two, four, eight, sixteen or 'n' slices, according to the frugality or industry of the Jungian dispenser. The whole system is reminiscent of the frame devised by a professor of the College of Laputa 'to improve speculative knowledge by practical mechanical operations'. At a turn of the forty handles, it will be remembered, the disposition of the inset words was completely changed, whereupon significant juxtapositions were read off and noted down by the scribes. Whether the Jungian framework was determined by a love of opposites or by an alchemical regard for the number four, it is not possible to say, although Jung's devotion to venerable numbers make the latter suggestion not wholly implausible. But however ingeniously we may multiply the patterns of conscious psychology, we cannot expect to glean more from our labours than we originally contributed. Conscious psychology is a closed circuit which we follow only to return to our starting point. It is not surprising therefore to find that whereas the words 'introvert' and 'extravert' have achieved dictionary rank and in polite circles have come to be used as handy terms of domestic abuse, the more complicated of Jung's character combinations have fallen on stony ground. Alchemy notwithstanding, an error cannot be rectified by multiplying its parts.

106

CHAPTER VI

DREAMS AND NEUROSES

THE reader who has endured a necessarily technical and too probably tedious discussion of the respective merits of Freudian and Jungian theories of mind, may well cry mercy at the prospect of hearing additional disputation concerning the nature of dreams and neuroses. He may feel that if, as the writer holds, Jung by his defection from Freudian principles reduced himself to the ranks of conscious and academic psychologists, there is no point in comparing Freudian with Jungian theories of dreams and of neuroses: no common ground can possibly exist between them. Nevertheless there are a number of reasons why he cannot be spared some consideration of these matters.

In the first place it is commonly believed that Jung's theory of dreams is deeper and loftier than that of Freud, in that Jung not only stresses the 'prospective function' of dreams but is convinced they harness to the service of the individual the imperishable wisdom of past ages; and of course it is a fact that Jung regards the dream as constituting a symbolic guide to present and future conduct. This is a view, incidentally, that could be maintained by the most superficial conscious psychologist, is indeed frequently maintained by sibyls of the kitchen and nursery. Similarly regarding the neuroses; it is commonly thought that by attributing the outbreak of neuroses to a conscious cause, namely, a failure on the part of the individual to achieve his life task, Jung discovered a more edifying motivation of mental disorder than a mere (Freudian) conflict between man's unconscious conscience and his primitive instincts. Clearly then an omission to discuss dreams and neuroses might be regarded as a pusillanimous evasion on the part of a Freudian commentator. In any case the reader who unthinkingly subscribes to the fashionable view according to

107

which Jung's psychology is in some way superior to that of Freud is not entitled to claim respite from scientific argument of the issue wherever it may lie or lead.

There is however a more cogent reason for the present course. The task of the psychologist is not discharged by giving a detailed account of mental structure, energies and mechanisms, or even by recording the processes that regulate human character. It must include also a description of the *total function of the psyche* and this account must throw some light on the unconscious problems and conscious perplexities of men, women and children. If man were not a conflict-ridden animal our interest in psychology would die of inanition. That the older academic psychologies were treated with contemptuous disregard by the intelligent public was due to the fact that these sterile handmaidens of metaphysics were blind to the universality of human conflict.

Now it was characteristic of the old psychologies that they treated man not only as a 'laboratory' subject and as a perpetual adult, but as if he were for ever sound in wind and limb and perpetually awake. These were grotesque assumptions. Even adults spend a third of their adult span of life asleep; sucklings, at a conservative estimate, threequarters of their infantile life. The lives of sucklings are a succession of eternities disturbed by fitful periods of eating and excreting, which only gradually lead to the measurement of time. In the second place although the incidence even of major mental diseases has never been exactly estimated, it is safe to say that anything from a third to threequarters of the race suffer from psychological malfunctions of one kind or another. A psychology which ignores the sleeping functions of the mind and the mental disorders of waking life is a snare and an illusion. It creates an illusion by fostering the impression that 'normality' is a God-like attribute. Dispassionately regarded the 'normal psychologist' is seen to be three parts theologian.

That dreams and neuroses are considered here under a single caption is not due simply to the need for compression.

108

Even from the descriptive point of view they have a great deal in common. A nightmaré of being hunted by some wild animal is accepted by most as a natural risk incident to falling asleep. A child's anxiety of animals is usually, although wrongly, discounted as a natural fear. But the animal phobia of an adult, although by general consent stigmatized as morbid, can legitimately be regarded as a dissociated fragment of dream life which has apparently been torn from its dream-bed to masquerade as part of real everyday life. Even closer is the structural resemblance between a dream and a symptom formation or symptomatic act. But this is to anticipate the technical argument; for to Jung the Freudian theory of dreams and symptom-formation is dictated by the personal ideosyncrasies of its founder, whereas to the Freudian Jung's theory of dreams and neuroses is a nonsense. Let us therefore in the first place consider them separately.

DREAMS. In these sophisticated times when it is taken for granted by all and sundry that dreams have something to do with psychology and when even the hard-bitten psychiatrist in his more reckless moods is ready to wager his respectability on a discreet dream interpretation, it is hard to realize how momentous were the issues that hung on Freud's discovery of their way and meaning. Yet it is no more than the sober truth to say that in the history of human understanding there have been but two fateful occasions. The first arose in the dawn of prehistory when man, all unwitting, developed that faculty of repression which, whether gradually or suddenly we cannot tell, shut off the dynamic unconscious from perceptual consciousness and by blocking the automatic action of the conditioned reflex gained time and psychic space for his Ego to develop. The other occurred towards the end of the nineteenth century when Freud, alone and unaided, crashed through the walls of the familiar to discover the unconscious mind.

109

How easy it would have been to follow the line of least resistance, to remain on the hither side of the repression barrier and leave the interpretation of dreams to physiologists and soothsayers. Indeed it is not beyond the bounds of possibility that the discovery of the unconscious may yet be lost. For the more Freud's theory of dreams is misapprehended or bowdlerized, and these are after all the tendencies of latter-day psychology, the more its foothold on modern science will slip. It is all the more significant therefore to recall that within almost a decade of the publication of Freud's work, one of the earliest and apparently most enthusiastic of his acolytes renounced his Freudian convictions and propounded a system of dream interpretation which reduced the dream process to the level of conscious ratiocination. Jung was indeed the first and greatest Bowdler in the annals of clinical psychology.

Although it is beyond the scope of this essay to marshall in detail the technical arguments involved, it is not hard to indicate the main points at issue and to indicate why, holding the views he did, Jung was compelled to abandon the technical process of *analysing* dreams and to revert to the more ancient practice of *reading* them. *For it will scarcely be denied that the popularity of Jung's dream psychology hangs on his conviction that dreams have a prospective tendency, that* THEY *can read the future as well as the present.* Now the essence of Freud's theory is that the *dream-work* as such performs no intellectual operation whatsoever. Dreamwork consists in the application of various mechanisms having the summated effect of *distorting* the *latent dream thoughts* so that they can pass the *dream censorship* in the disguised form which is observed in the *manifest content* of a dream. The latent dream thoughts may be derived from the pre-conscious as well as the true unconscious system although it is the conflict aroused by certain unconscious presentations which activates the censorship, and consequently instigates the dream-work. And naturally the range of preconscious thinking is as extensive in sleep as
110

in waking life. The (pre)conscious can look forward as far as the mind's eye can see.

Another source of rational dream thinking, including thoughts about the present and future, is provided by the process of *secondary elaboration*, whereby the disjointed manifest content is linked up, varnished over and usually though not invariably, given an appearance of connected thinking. Secondary elaborations are essentially 'after thoughts' intended to make good any failure on the part of the dream-work to disguise the disturbing and conflict-inducing unconscious impulses of the dreamer. And as they occur at the point of waking they have practically the whole range of intellectual operations at their disposal. *Closely examined, Jung's prospective tendency is for the most part a manifestation of secondary elaboration differing in no way from the waking processes of introspection and ratiocination.* This is borne out by the fact that Jungian prospective interpretations differ in no way from candid comments on the personality and potentialities of the dreamer such as might be offered him for his own good by any officious friend.

This misconception of the nature of dreaming is extremely widespread. It is true of course that dream life is the way our mind works during sleep; and it might be said rather loosely that the dream provides us with a peephole through which we can inspect the workings of the unconscious. But it is a window of bottle glass which also distorts the inner scene beyond ordinary recognition. The manifest content of a dream brings us no nearer to unconscious activity than do the bizarre products of the schizophrenic imagination or the more calculated preciosities of the surrealist. What we actually see in the manifest content is the *result* of a conflict between the wish to sleep and any stimuli that threaten to disturb sleep; and of these disturbing excitations the most constant and turbulent are repressed wishes. Not just sexual wishes, as is commonly averred by non-analysts, but any unconscious impulse which incurs the disapproval of the super-ego or unconscious conscience. As however the

111

physical immobility of the dreamer encourages a bolder advance on the part of the unconscious, the dream is inevitably a *compromise formation in which unconscious wishfulfilments are permitted in the form of harmless hallucinations;* the latent thoughts are dramatised and illustrated in visual images, which however are modified beyond recognition by the repressing forces.

Once the significance of 'dream-work' has been grasped, it is not hard to recognize the fundamental error in Jung's method of interpretation. To put it quite simply *Jung by ignoring the existence of dream-work confuses the manifest with the latent content of the dream.* His readings of dreams are no more profound than the alternative readings of Calphurnia's dream in *Julius Cæsar*.

> *Cæsar:* Calphurnia here, my wife, stays me at home
> She dreamt tonight she saw my statua,
> Which, like a fountain with an hundred spouts,
> Did run pure blood, and many lusty Romans
> Came smiling and did bathe their hands in it:
> And these does she apply for warnings and portents,
> And evils imminent. . . .

The conspirator, it will be remembered, for reasons of his own, immediately produces a more subtle and yet more obviously tendentious interpretation:

> *Decius:* This dream is all amiss interpreted;
> It was a vision fair and fortunate:
> Your statue spouting blood in many pipes,
> In which so many smiling Romans bath'd,
> Signifies that from you great Rome shall suck
> Reviving blood . . .
> This by Calphurnia's dream is signified.

> *Cæsar:* And this way have you well expounded it.

The dream, being Calphurnia's, though related by Cæsar, raises, of course, no prophetic issue in the Jungian sense; since in Jung's system it is the dreamer, aided by the analyst, who prophesies *his own fate*; the interpretations are simply preconscious readings of symbolism dictated by the conscious reactions and motives of the respective 'analysts'. No doubt Jungian readings are more amusing to the patient and in the long run more flattering to his vanity than the dynamic interpretations of the Freudian school but they can give no possible hint as to the latent content of any dream. The Jungian symbol by definition can have no latent content, and the conscious content speaks for itself. With the obliteration of dream-work, dream interpretation reverts to augury.

Admittedly Freud's functional approach to dream psychology, involving as it does the concept of the dynamic unconscious, of the primary processes that govern the unconscious system, of a repression-barrier, of the super-ego or unconscious conscience, of unconscious conflict and of unconscious resistance, is inevitably disappointing to those who seek hopefully in dreams for evidence of man's occult and magical powers. Having been deprived of any satisfactions of this kind in the field of physical science and finding no very convincing evidence for them in conscious activities, they are loath to abandon the view that the dream is the work of a far-seeing 'mentor' endowed with vitalising energies, whose primary concern it is to see that men fulfil their individual and racial destinies. To such expectant observers it must bring precious comfort to have Jung's reassurance that the dream can be 'a mysterious message from our night-aspect', an oracular pronouncement pointing to inner and outer dangers and indicating the appropriate solution of the difficulty. The dream, says Jung, represents the inner truth and reality 'as it is and not as I suppose it to be, and also not as I should like to have it'. The manifest content, adds Jacobi, shews 'what the unconscious has to say about the situation in question . . . *always saying exactly what it means*'. (Author's italics.) Even when it is expressed in the archaic symbols of the Collective Unconscious it points a moral, the moral of individuation. However much it may talk the language of infantile or primitive thinking, it

113

continues those processes of reflection and introspection which ought to be but are not fully applied to any given problem by the conscious mind. The dream is therefore in the first instance 'the subliminal picture of the psychological condition of the individual in his waking state'. These are assumptions which the man in the street, accustomed to practise what he calls 'sleeping on' his problems, will no doubt regard as entirely sensible and adequate.

So much for the *teleological function* of the Jungian dream. When we come to consider Jung's views on the *processes* of dream formation we find the same complete confusion of ideas which pervades his general theory of mind. Using terms which have a Freudian sound but which have lost their Freudian meaning, Jung gives the impression that his dream psychology is not entirely divorced from that of Freud, but at the same time describes dream mechanisms that are incompatible not only with Freudian theory but with his own assumptions. In Jung's view analysis leads into the 'land of childhood', a period when rational consciousness was not yet separated from the Collective Unconscious. Here apparently the Personal Unconscious with its infantile problems and complexes mingles somewhat with the prehistoric unconscious. Indeed it sometimes appears as if Jung thought the road to the Collective Unconscious lay through the Personal Unconscious. The adult having lost contact with this 'land of childhood' experiences a 'want of instinct' and feels disoriented in general human situations. The result is that the 'land of childhood' remains infantile, and its childish inclinations, being unwelcome to consciousness, are 'repressed'. Life is dried up and can regain its vitality only in the 'land of childhood' where directions can be received from the unconscious. To experience the unconscious is however, according to Jung, 'beyond the courage as well as the ability of the average occidental'.

Now, disregarding the confusion caused by indiscriminate use of the word unconscious, all this theorizing is entirely opposed to the Jungian view that the dream continues the processes of conscious introspection and reflection. Talk of repression merely confounds confusion. In fact Jung specifically rejects the Freudian concept of *dream-censorship*. And what is dream-censorship but the mechanism whereby repression is activated? Why bother even to mention the repressed, if there is no such thing as repression; *if there is no dream-censorship then repression does not exist*. Nor does the confusion end here. Jung introduces into his dream psychology the principle of compensation and complementariness. So that 'only from the knowledge of the conscious situation is it possible to settle what sign is to be given to the unconscious contents'. Hence the value of symbols varies; some, Jung admits, are fixed; but the majority, he maintains, are not; their content can be determined only by their relation to the individual situation. Even the influence of conscious type-psychology is taken into account; dreams can be distinguished by the part played in their formation by functional characteristics both of consciousness and of the Collective Unconscious.

Needless to say the points selected for consideration here are only samples of Jung's dream theory: they are however sufficiently representative to indicate the general trend of his system and to illustrate the confusions and contradictions which are so characteristic of Jung's theoretical presentations. Thus, dreams are spontaneous products of the unconscious, peculiar and autonomous. They must therefore be, like the Collective Unconscious from which they spring, neutral in the moral sense and devoid of intellectual judgment. Yet apparently they are capable of returning unfavourable verdicts on the current state of consciousness. They are archaic products, yet their archaic meaning cannot be read except in terms of current life. 'Every dream' says Jung 'is a means of information and control'. Being autonomous they cannot be influenced by consciousness or even dream-consciousness: yet by the Jungian laws of compensation they can be very decisively influenced by the conscious system. Sexual symbols have ultimately a non-sexual

115

significance. Dreams are unorganized: yet they are organized. Dreams never deceive: we deceive ourselves. The existence of 'repressed' material modifies their form: yet Jung can see no sign of repression *in* the dream. The phantasies of the Collective Unconscious contained in dreams are derived, we are told, from archaic tendencies inherited at birth; yet the patient alone determines their interpretation and no interpretation can be regarded as correct which does not induce in the patient 'a vital feeling of assent'.

But does the patient alone determine their interpretation? By no means. For after a preliminary phase the Jungian analyst takes a hand in the processes of 'amplification' and 'assimilation'. By amplification is meant a broadening and enrichment of the dream-content 'with all possible similar analogous images'. 'It is further distinguished from free association' says Jacobi 'in that the associations are contributed not only by the patient or dreamer but also by the physician', who often 'determines the direction that the associations of the patient may take'. In other words Jung who prides himself on avoiding the reductive 'Why' of Freud, and on substituting the not essentially different question 'To what purpose', sees to it that a Jungian purpose is found. Yet in almost the same breath he maintains that his dream analysis is not suggestion.

Similarly with 'assimilation'. By assimilation Jung means 'a mutual interpenetration of conscious and unconscious thoughts'. As soon as the patient begins to assimilate the contents that were previously unconscious 'the danger from the side of the unconscious diminishes'. And, as has already been noted, Jung believes that the unconscious is dangerous only when our conscious attitude to it becomes 'dangerously false'. The correction of this false attitude in included in the work of dream interpretation; the patient is instructed in mythology by the Jungian analyst. This again happens in the more advanced phases of analysis or at any rate after the (Jungian) Personal Unconscious has been voided of its complexes, when the 'true' meaning of the neurosis or character difficulty is about to emerge. In other words assimilation, in principle a subjective process, is made an excuse for forcible feeding. *Here is yet another clue to the tendency of Jung's psychology*. Scratch a Russian, it is said, and you will find a Tartar. Scratch man and you will find a child; so runs the psychological variant of the proverb. Studying Jung, one is tempted to add yet another version : scratch the psychologist and you will find a pedagogue.

But perhaps it would be better to allow Jung himself to pass judgement on these matters. 'I have' he says 'no dream theory. I do not know how dreams came about. I am also completely uncertain whether or not my way of dealing with dreams deserves to be called a "method".' In fact he is ready 'to construct a totally new theory of dreams from every single case'. And 'if it were not so paradoxical' he would be tempted to issue this warning to the prospective interpreter of dreams: 'do anything you like, only do not try to understand'. A paradox, it would appear, holds no terror for Jung.

NEUROSES. To the casual observer it may not be at all apparent why it is necessary to drag the neuroses into any discussion of psychological theories. Surely, he may argue, mental disorders indicate at most some deficiency, conceivably even some exaggeration of mental function, but nothing that would throw any light on the essential nature of mind. Hence the common reproach, levelled, interestingly enough, more against Freud than against Jung, that mental theories based on clinical psychology are bound to be both inadequate and distorted if not indeed perverted. In this connection it is not without significance that Jung's period of enthusiastic devotion to Freud's theories coincided with his own psychiatric phase, i.e., the time when his attention was directed mainly towards the insanities; and

117

that later developments of the Jungian system occurred at a time when, to judge from Jung's own comments, the majority of his patients had very little the matter with them, save some 'problem in individuation'.

This common misapprehension of the nature of mental disorder is a perpetual stumbling-block to psychological understanding. To realize the function of mind it is necessary to grasp two essential facts: first, that in both descriptive and developmental senses, mental phenomena can be arranged in well-defined series; and second, that the master mechanism of mental illness is an unconscious regression which in its backward sweep activates in reverse order the early phases of development and is arrested only at the point of maximal infantile 'fixation'. An illustration of the serial approach is the view that a dream is a manifestation of 'normal' insanity occurring during the behaviouristically 'safe' hours of sleep; also that a psychosis, such as schizophrenic insanity, is a 'normal' dream persisting throughout waking life. In fact we can arrange a descriptive series of mental phenomena, ordering them in terms of their relation to objective reality. Starting with the dreams of normal persons and the hallucinations and delusions of the insane and continuing by way of the conflict-producing phantasies and illusions of neurotics or the pathological lies and deceptions of delinquent types, we reach finally the day dreams of everyman, the imaginative products of the artist and, by way of contrast, the logical thought of the scientist.

Even more significant is the developmental series. Make a cross-section of the mentality of the average child of two and a half to three and a half years and you will find patterns of thought and behaviour which are akin to those of an adult suffering from the rituals and compulsive thoughts of an obsessional neurosis. Hence the importance of the fixation point, namely, the stage of mental development at which either the instincts of the child or its ego functions are partially arrested, and at which, given a sufficiently

118

serious regression, the processes of *symptom-formation* originate. The symptoms we observe are merely end-products varying in depth according to the fixation point or points determined during childhood development. By studying these symptom products we secure an insight into the normal development of mind which totally eludes the student of normal psychology. We can see the neuroses and psychoses not as bizarre and incomprehensible artefacts disturbing the normal tenour of our adult ways but as caricatures of early phases of development, as it were turned inside out.

If we accept these essentially Freudian views of mental disorder, we must also examine the dynamic factors responsible for the symptom process. And this can best be done by studying the beginning and end of the regression series. It soon becomes apparent that not only are infantile fixation points associated with experiences of frustration but that the precipitating factors or exciting causes of adult mental disorder lie in frustration whether obvious or occult, traumatic or summated. Partial or total frustration leads to a varying degree of withdrawal of (Freudian) libido from its reality objects and the reflux of libido, pursuing a regressive path, reaches the fixation point, thereby charging the weakest part of the mental apparatus with an excessive amount of energy. To put the matter a little too schematically, the charges of regression meet with the forward-driving charges of unconscious and repressed instincts. Repression breaks down under the strain and the unconscious ego, bowing to necessity, seeks to effect a *compromise* between the ineffectively repressed and the ineffectively repressing forces. *This constitutes the process of symptom-formation.* In a sense therefore the neurosis is an attempted self-cure which salves the major part of the ego at the cost of local disruption, an attempt which 'fails' precisely because of this disruption.

It will be seen therefore that in Freudian theory the main mechanisms of dream-formation and symptom-formation

119

are identical. In both cases regression occurs, in both cases a conflict exists between the forces of the unconscious and the repressing forces; in both cases an attempt is made to solve the problem by unconscious compromise formation, by which however the true nature of the unconscious impulses is denied. By way of contrast the normal person is either resistant to frustration or has a more effective repression system or utilises his mental mechanisms in such a way as to prevent undue damning up of mental energy. Behind this normal facade however the mind of the normal person works with the same forces, the same structures, the same mechanisms. We are all brothers under the skin.

Those who have followed the outline of Jung's general theory of mind, and of his theory of dreams should have no difficulty in forecasting his theory of neuroses. For example, if there is no dream censorship and therefore no latent content causing conflict, it follows that neuroses cannot be the result of unconscious conflict between instinctual forces and the forces at the disposal of the unconscious ego. Neither can symptoms have any structure. The relation of the Collective Unconscious to ego-consciousness must be a directly reactive one in which consciousness has at least as much say as the unconscious. Moreover there can be no *processes of symptom formation*, no compromise products. Unlike the Freudian unconscious, the Jungian Collective Unconscious has no economic processes of its own. Whether the archetypes are ideational forms charged with energy or merely inherited energic tendencies, and according to Jung both propositions are true, they derive their significance only from their immediate impact on ego-consciousness. Moreover if dreams have a prospective tendency concerned with the achievement of a life-task, and if the archetypes revitalize ego-consciousness, it follows that one of the main causes if not the main cause of neurosis must be a failure on the part of consciousness to perform the life-task of the individual. If

120

however archetypes are revitalizing, a neurosis should under certain circumstances be a desirable contingency. Moreover if consciousness is responsible for the neurosis, we need not expect to find any evidence of faulty repression. Rather we must expect the fault to lie with the character of the individual, some timidity or cowardice that leads him to turn his back simultaneously on the task of life and on the constitutional tendencies of the Collective Unconscious.

Further information as to Jungian theories of the neurosis can be obtained from a study of Jung's methods of dream interpretation. As we have seen Jung's attitude so far from being analytic is ultimately pedagogic. And, to add to our list of psychological proverbs, we have only to scratch the pedagogue to find the moralist, the moral suasionist and sooner or later the occupational therapeutist. The Jungian pedagogue and the Jungian moral suasionist may protest that they are only following the directions of the patient's Collective Unconscious. But they protest in vain. The physician who takes a part in *shaping* his patient's life policies commits himself to the view that he knows better than the patient what is good for him, and, if he should happen to be a Jungian physician, that he knows better than the patient's Collective Unconscious. He also believes that the solution of mental disorder lies in consciousness, a view which does no more than echo the hoary injunction served on the patient by both family and friends that he should 'pull himself together.'

A brief survey of Jungian formulations on the subject of neuroses confirms these conjectures, adding to them merely a number of contradictory statements which increase the general confusion. Incidentally it is remarkable how very little either Jung or his followers have to say on the subject. To be sure, the term 'neurosis' is frequently used but in little more than a descriptive sense, as often as not a synonym for conscious perturbation over trifles. This procedure is logical enough : for if, as Jung confesses, he has no dream theory, neither can he have a theory of neurosis. Hence no

121

doubt the multiplicity of definitions stressing the purely conscious nature of its causes.

The story commences with an official recantation. 'Therefore I no longer find the cause of the neurosis in the past, but in the present. I ask what the necessary task is which the patient will not accomplish.' As the result of this dereliction of duty the patient's libido regresses into the unconscious where it may find fresh inspiration to surmount the obstacle. If it does not and if his libido merely reactivates earlier or infantile patterns, a neurosis develops. By way of variety neurosis is described as the 'suffering of a human being, who has not discovered what life means to him,' or, 'an act of adaptation that has failed'. Veering slightly from this environmental theory, Jung also maintains that a neurosis is a 'dissociation of the personality due to the existence of complexes', i.e., psychic constellations of content having emotional tone. A delicious compromise between environmental and endopsychic factors is found in the statement that 'a neurosis is an attempt to compensate for the one-sidedness of the conscious attitude which led to the neurosis'. From this point onwards the positive and creative aspects of the Jungian neurosis begin to emerge. The neurosis 'forces the patient to adopt a new attitude'. Endopsychic factors are increasingly accentuated. The neurosis is 'a protection against the inner activity of the psyche', an attempt 'to escape from the inner voice and from vocation' . . . . 'Behind the neurotic perversion is concealed vocation, destiny, the development of personality, the complete realization of the life-will that is born with the individual.' When we enquire what this inner voice is, we are told 'the voice of a fuller life.' So ultimately neurosis is defined as a tearing in two of the 'inner self'.

The obvious fact is that having recanted his Freudian theories, Jung is compelled to recant his recantation and doesn't mind doing so provided the withdrawal is amply covered by a smoke-screen of Jungian equivocations. Thus neuroses 'are only partly due to infantile predisposition'. In

122

some cases, including that of Freud himself, the Freudian
theory of neurosis is regarded as valid and, particularly in
young people, a Freudian approach may be appropriate, by
which apparently is implied that the patient's 'sexual problems' should be given an airing. On the other hand we are
told that there is 'nothing specific for neurosis in these infantile phantasies'. The neurotic, Jung says, has 'infantile
conflicts' and is markedly influenced by 'infantile phantasies' and 'by the peculiar use he makes of his infantile past'.
Nevertheless the sexual theory of neurosis, whatever that
means to Jung, is 'too narrow' . . . 'an energic viewpoint'
must be substituted. 'The mentality of the neurotic is *basic-
ally* normal.' On the other hand Jung would not let the
patient think *'his own overwhelming powers'* cause the neurosis. It is *'much better'* if he understands that his complex is an
Autonomous Power directed against his conscious personality.

But let us, for mercy's sake, gloss over these contradictions; let us assume for the sake of argument that the
cause of the neurosis lies at that part of the conscious mind
which impinges on environment, for where else can we conceive the psychic location of a 'life-task'. What, we may ask,
is this life task, failure to perform which causes the neurosis? And why does the neurotic fail to perform it? Jung's
answer is that circumstances become too much for the
patient's power of, or will to, adaptation. The circumstances
need not be anything uncommon, dramatic or traumatic:
the patient may be merely unsatisfactory, e.g., to his parents
and himself: a poor, unprogressive figure: his mentality may
sink in this way or that: or he may remain entangled with
his family, in which case the symptoms may take the form
of regression to some (Freudian) fixation point.   In any case
these infantile phantasies are of no particular moment and
should be 'pulled up'.

But why does the patient not adapt to these commonplace circumstances? Because, to condense Jung's views on
anxiety, he is scared by the demands of adaptation. And why
is he scared? At this point Jung throws his own theory to the

winds. *Because he is 'congenitally sensitive'.* Now since the conscious 'precipitating' cause is banal, and since the neurosis must not have its predisposing cause in childhood, we are forced to assume either that it has no cause worth mentioning or that the essential cause is constitutional, i.e., an inherited tendency. Further, since the Collective Unconscious is the respository of all inherited psychic tendencies, it follows that the cause of the neurosis lies not just in the present day, not just in superficial layers of consciousness, but in the Collective Unconscious, that is it say the in deepest part. As is his custom, Jung insists on having it both ways.

It has been suggested earlier that Jung's theory of neuroses could have been inferred from his theory of dreams. To this it can now be added that the fundamental fallacy in his theory of neurosis is identical with the fallacy underlying his dream theory. Being first and last a conscious psychologist, Jung confuses the *manifest* content with the *latent* content of the dream. Similarly in the case of the neurosis. Constitutional elements apart, the neurosis has, according to Jung's system, *no latent content.* To be sure Freud insisted that the manifest content of the dream is subject to secondary (preconscious) elaboration which seeks to give the dream a plausible present-day reference: but he was never deceived by this superficial defensive process. Similarly Freud pointed out that the symptom-formation, although elaborated in the unconscious system, could be exploited by the (pre)conscious system for purposes of immediate gain. This 'secondary gain from illness' enables the patient, for example, to establish a favoured position amongst his family or friends: or to avoid tasks of immediate adaptation which are distasteful to him. *But the secondary gain from a neurosis should not be confused with its primary cause.* Jung could not or would not recognise this elementary distinction. The 'prospective tendency' he attributes to neurosis is a consequence not a cause. So far from being a contribution to unconscious psychology, Jung's theory of the neurosis constitutes a regression to pre-Freudian academic psychology.

124

In fact Jung has contributed nothing to unconscious psychology except the term 'complex', a concept which incidentally has now been replaced by more detailed and specific labels. It is not surprising therefore to find that Jungian therapy is essentially a process of moral education. If neuroses are due to a conscious and deliberate failure to perform 'tasks', treatment should logically take the form of pedagogic guidance. And this, as we shall see, is precisely what Jungian analysis is. The correction of the neurosis in is Jung's own words 'a highly moral task of immense educational value'.

CHAPTER VII

INDIVIDUATION : THE JUNGIAN ODYSSEY

SHOULD the reader's patience have been taxed by this prolonged survey of the technical and theoretical aspects of the Freud-Jung controversy he will no doubt urge that it is high time the issue was presented in terms of everyday life and value. He may insist that after all the best test of any psychological system is its applicability to the practical problems of life from the cradle to the grave. And although a good deal turns on the meaning he attaches to the term 'problem', the challenge is one that no self-respecting psychologist would dream of evading, even were it possible. One of Jung's stock accusations against psycho-analysis is that by the use of 'reductive' analysis the creative values of the individual are grossly neglected in the Freudian system. This charge Jung seeks to make good, first of all by issuing a special definition of the term 'individual' and then trying to prove that the main problem of life is to attain a state of 'individuation'.

Before entering this fresh field of controversy it is well to familiarise oneself with the Jungian 'stages of life'. The exact number of these stages seems to vary. At times it would appear that he follows a rough biological outline distinguishing a pre-sexual phase, a sexual phase and a phase of sexual disintegration manifesting itself in a regression towards the pre-sexual phase. But in the long run his sacred regard for the number four prevails and the 'one hundred and eighty degrees of the arc of life are divisible into four parts': childhood, youth, middle life and senescence. Although this involves Jung in a subdivision of childhood into a nutritional and a prepubertal phase and extends youth to the age limit of 35—40, a period during which most individuals have completed the reproductive phase of family life, we need not cavil over the number of stages. The crux of the matter lies in the existence or non-existence

126

during the various stages of characteristic 'problems'. In childhood, that is to say from birth to puberty, we are, according to Jung, a problem for others but are not yet conscious of any problems of our own; we become conscious of problems throughout youth and middle-age; in old age, unworried by problems of our own 'we become something of a problem to others', and, like children, are submerged in unconscious psychic happenings. This is the quintessence of the Jungian system which if not an all-time record for banality and wilful neglect of the facts of life, will at least come as something of a surprise to our forty-year-olds to say nothing of our more robust and expectant septuagenarians.

It is tempting to linger awhile on these 'stages'. There are says Jung, no problems without consciousness. So we may legitimately infer that unconscious conflict does not exist, a conclusion which, as we have seen, follows in any case from a study of his general theory and of his theory of dreams and neuroses. The child has no problems because it is 'still enclosed in the psychic atmosphere of its parents', the conscious distinction of the ego from the parents takes place at puberty, a view which the learned Lipsius, to say nothing of Grotius and John Stuart Mill, would certainly have resented. If however it be true, not only is there no unconscious conscience (super-ego) in childhood, but no conscious alter-ego until adult sexuality develops. The child, says Jung, merely recognizes or knows. Yet even here there are contradictions. The ego, he says, is first consciously perceived at puberty: nevertheless, he maintains, in childhood the child does develop a feeling of 'I-ness'. To continue: the problems of youth arise mainly because youth clings to childish illusions. It follows therefore that the turbulence of sexual development is only a secondary cause of the problems of youth. In any case these, says Jung, can best be solved by 'attainment, usefulness and so forth'. 'The serious problems of life however are never fully solved' (at this stage). Though he stretches youth to cover what was once the average expectation of life, Jung is clearly no youth fan.

127

At middle age we are not much better off. Our achievements have been bought at the price of 'a diminution of personality'. 'The wine of youth . . . often times grows turbid.' We are one-sided and tend to become rigid between 40 and 50 years of age. We cling to our youth, as the youth clings to his childhood. Also we change in our sexual constitution: masculine becomes feminine and feminine, masculine. This is a tardy repentance on Jung's part. Having previously blunted our imagination with a functional and attitudinal type-psychology and confused our understanding with the *anima-us-i* formations of the Collective Unconscious which are at the same time archetypes, reactive manifestations of the contra-sexual and non-sexual manifestations of the libido, we are now told that manifest sexual factors play an important role in middle-age. In any case, the difficulty is apparently settled by the advent of senility, when however a new problem poses itself: how to die gracefully. 'It is hygienic,' says Jung, 'to discover in death a goal towards which one can strive.' Hence, to quote his typically evasive formulations, 'I . . . consider the religious teaching of a life hereafter *consonant with the standpoint of psychic hygiene*' (Author's italics). . . . 'The ancient *athanasius pharmakon*, the medicament of immortality is more profound and meaningful than we supposed.'

We are now in a position to follow the Jungian Odyssey of *individuation*. This process, says Jung, consists in the 'realization of self-hood' and 'is not just a mental problem but the problem of life itself'. It is a centralising process, the production of 'a new centre of the personality'. This centre is also called the *self*—'a term that is meant to include the totality of the psyche in so far as this manifests itself in an individual'. 'The self,' he goes on, 'is not only the centre but also the circumference that encloses consciousness and the unconscious: it is the centre of this totality, as the ego is the centre of consciousness.' Wholeness of the personality involves a differentiation of the pairs of opposites, a 'joining together' of the conscious and unconscious parts of the total

128

psyche which thenceforward stand in 'a living relation' to one another. 'Only he who can deliberately say "yes" to the power of the destiny* he finds within him becomes a personality.'

Lest the unwary reader should imagine that this main problem of life can be solved by the unaided efforts of ordinary mortals travelling through its various stages, Jung takes care to qualify his position in a number of ways. The unconscious, he points out, can never be made completely conscious and always possesses the greater store of energy. Hence 'the personality as a full realization of the wholeness of our being is an unattainable ideal'. The idea of the self is moreover only a borderline concept, as, e.g., the *Ding an sich* of Kant. It is a 'transcendental' postulate, and indication of that in the psyche which is 'primary and unfathomable'. It is also an ethical postulate, a goal for realization. 'It is,' says Jacobi, 'that focal point of our psyche in which God's image shows itself most plainly.'

If further discouragement be needed it is to be found in the statement that the establishment of the wholeness of the personality is a task of middle life (i.e. from 35—40 onwards) and is a preparation for death. The first half of life is unsuitable for the task, since the individual spends or should spend that period in adjustment to the external world. Only in middle life, our young sophomores will be

* K. W. Bash, translating Jacobi's *Die Psychologie von C. G. Jung*, renders her quotation from Jung as above. S. Dell, translating the original of *The Integration of the Personality*, gives the passage as 'Only the man who is able *consciously* to affirm the power of the vocation confronting him from within becomes a personality'; and throughout the chapter Dell translates *Bestimmung* as vocation. Actually the rendering of Bash is to be preferred. The meaning Jung gives to 'vocation' is closer to 'destiny' in the sense of fate (*Geschick*) than to 'calling' in the sense of *beruf*. As will be seen, Jung regards *Bestimmung* as an irrational factor, acting like a law of God from which there is no escape, an inner voice calling, an objective fate 'hard as granite and heavy as lead . . . saying to him in an audible (sic) voice "This is what will and must happen".' Jung while objecting to Freudian concepts of *psychic determinism* is evidently prepared to preach *predestination*, a fact which Jacobi's translator has evidently grasped.

129

surprised to learn, can true perfection be attained. This self-realization is however granted to few. Indeed, the road is not suitable or traversible for everyone. 'It is also,' says Jacobi, 'not without danger, and it requires the strictest control by the associate or physician as well as by one's own consciousness to maintain the integrity of the ego against the violently inbreaking contents of the unconscious. . . .' 'The attempt to go such a journey alone . . . would be perilous for the Occidental if it succeeded at all.' Try not the pass, the (Occidental) old man said.

The cat is now almost out of the bag. Spontaneous individuation is not for the mob but for rare creative spirits of middle age. For all lesser and younger spirits, that is to say for the majority of mankind, the only hope is artificial individuation, and this, we are led to infer, can only be attained through Jungian analysis. 'The process of individuation,' says Jacobi, 'is an intense analytical effort which concentrates with strictest integrity and under the direction of consciousness, upon the internal psychological process . . . hacking through layer upon layer to that centre which is the source and ultimate ground of our psychic existence— to the inner core, the Self.' And this after we have been expressly warned that the Self is made not born.

Needless to say the process of individuation can be described only with the help of Jungian archetypes. First, we experience the *shadow*, that symbol of our 'other aspect' or 'dark brother'. Here we meet our undifferentiated function and rudimentarily developed attitude, which at the same time represent that 'primordial disposition' which we reject 'because it stands in contradiction to our conscious principles'. We can be objective about our own personality only when we have learned to distinguish ourselves from this shadow which is nevertheless already split off, a 'focal point' of the Collective Unconscious and an 'indissoluble archetype' derived from racial experience. Here, incidentally, we have the most direct and convincing evidence that Jung has completely abandoned the concept of unconscious 'conflict'.

Next we meet with the *soul-image* or *anima-us-i*, the contra-sexual. This 'habitual internal attitude', being projected, we experience 'in the other person'. Nevertheless it mediates between the ego and the inner world. The anima and the *persona* (or 'habitual external attitude') exist in compensatory relation. 'If the persona is intellectual, the soul-image is quite certainly sentimental.' It is urgently necessary to free oneself from the one or the other 'as soon' says Jacobi 'as the individual is no longer able to distinguish himself from them': though why this is necessary is not clear, the less so as the man's anima has an 'iridescent character' and 'elfin nature', and the woman's animus (i) is represented by 'something like an assemblage of fathers and other authorities who pronounce *ex cathedra* incontestable "sensible" judgements'. The most cogent reason in the case of the man appears to be that if his anima remains in the dark 'It thereupon becomes projected, and so the hero comes under his wife's thumb'. Anyhow, these archetypes are made conscious, and projected energies thereby freed for conscious use. Apparently the man is then unable to 'fall in love' but will be capable of deeper 'love'. This, of course, after the age of 35—40.

Once this has been achieved the individual makes a new reckoning and a new definition of his position. A new goal-tendency is signalized by the appearance in man of the archetype of the 'Wise Old Man' and in women of that of the 'Magna Mater' or great earth-mother which representing 'the cold and objective truth of nature', as if to say that the actual mother is not part of nature. According to Jacobi these primordial images represent in man materialized spirit, in woman matter impregnated with spirit. Man is essentially determined by spirit, woman by matter. When these archetypes are made conscious, man is for the second time liberated from the father, woman from the mother : they begin to perceive their own unique individuality, and become, in Jung's words, 'united with God in a spiritual childhood'.

The climax is now at hand. The 'persona', that step-child of the Jungian consciousness, has been 'dissolved'. The Collective Unconscious has been 'vanquished'. At the same time it has been 'united' with the conscious though a 'common mid-point'. Man becomes whole through self-realization. We have only to concentrate on this centre point, resisting all 'cowardly identifications', and the Self is born. A transvaluation of all values takes place. This is called 'transformation'. Our actions must henceforward correspond to the Self. Consciousness is broadened and deepened and the individual is placed 'in unconditional, binding and indissoluble community with' the object, the outer world.

To be sure there are difficulties. There is 'no objective criterion' of the state of individuation. The only content of the Self we know is the ego. 'The individuated ego feels itself an object of an unknown and superordinated subject.' We can only *experience* the Self. If however we can convert this Something 'that lies beyond the capacity of our understanding' into 'a new centre of gravity of the individual', a personality arises that suffers only in the 'lower levels' but in 'upper levels' is 'peculiarly detached from every sorrowful and joyful event alike'. The birth of this superior personality is symbolized in the *idea* of the Christian act of baptism, not however in the single magical rite of baptism. Spiritual man is born. The moment of birth is signalized by the appearance of the archetypical unifying symbol, or primordial image of psychic totality, known in the East as the *Mandala* or, as one might say, the 'magic enclosure'.

The résumé of Jung's theory of individuation given above, although extremely condensed, actually does more than justice to his presentation. It is impossible to convey to the reader who has not worked his way through Jungian literature the immense wordiness, confusion, contradictoriness and nebulosity of Jung's ideas on individuation. In-

deed it is impossible to subject them to systematic examination unless one distinguishes clearly between (*a*) formulations that, whether true or false, have at any rate some
psychological reference, (*b*) views of life that are merely
subjective prejudices, and (*c*) random thoughts that are
apparently introduced either because they have just occurred to him or because he believes they will create an impression of profundity.

As far as technical matters are concerned it is unnecessary either to repeat the criticisms already advanced concerning Jung's concepts of the Collective Unconscious, the
shadow, the anima (-us-i) the persona, the ego, or to point
again the absence of any intelligible relation between
his Collective Unconscious and Ego-consciousness. Jung's
outline of individuation merely throws into bolder relief the
poverty and mutual incompatibility of his concepts. It also
serves to indicate the main source of his confusion regarding
mental function. Jung has indulged in the luxury of backing
two horses running in opposite directions in the same race.
Being essentially a conscious psychologist, he is bound in the
long run to make ego-consciousness the centre of his system.
But having at the same time created the idea of the Collective Unconscious with its inexhaustible store of energy and
potential or actual wisdom, he is clearly at a loss to know
what to do with his Frankenstein monster. So he rings the
changes between asserting its perpetual neutral power, emphasizing its 'sensible' influence on the ego and indicating
the desirability of its 'vanquishment'; once vanquished it is
however *brought to life* again in a new disguise, namely, the
concept of a transcendental Self. This Self-concept corresponds to no ego-entity. Although it is both centre and circumference of the total psyche it can only be experienced
and only in part, a characteristic which originally Jung attributed to the Collective Unconscious alone. And what does
this new Self which we can only partly experience do for us?
Apart from reducing us to a milk and water state of contemplation of the outer world it binds us 'unconditionally and

133

indissolubly' to this outer world at a stage of life when according to Jung's own reckoning our main task should be to prepare for death, i.e., the final abandonment of our instinctual relations with the world of objects. But let Jung himself have the last word on the psychological utility of the self-concept. Since the 'real existence (of the self) can be confirmed by no external criterion: therefore too is every further attempt at description and explanation useless . . .'. And there we may leave this 'magnitude superordinate to the conscious ego'.

But although the Jungian concept of the individuated Self is psychologically useless, Jung's ideas on individuation and on the stages of life deserve to be studied closely if only for the light they throw on the origins of his whole system. It requires no great perspicacity to see that they are a mishmash of Oriental philosophy with a bowdlerized psychobiology. His stages of life bear a remarkable resemblance to that Eastern *curriculum vitæ* according to which the young man listens and learns, attains ripe manhood, raises a family, fulfils his social duties, turns in the third stage of life from mundane pursuits to seek the treasures of the inner (spiritual) world, having found which, he waits his end in the fourth stage in a state of passivity.[1]

[1] In this connection, Jung's view that in the fourth of their life-stages, old men and women, having apparently abandoned the ineluctable virtues of individuation, merge again in the Collective Unconscious from which as infants they derived their consciousness, suggests an interpretation of the *quasi-sacred mandala* entirely different from that suggested by Jung; it has in fact a simple ontogenetic, infantile origin and function. Mandalas are no more mystical or sacred than squares, circles, numbers or the legs of chairs to which infants cling with an apelike appreciation of their primitive utility. Even if we ignore entirely the unconscious (latent infantile) symbolism of the circle, it still has a satisfying pre-conscious explanation in the arms that encircle the infant. Mandalas need cause no more excitement than the framed photographs of the local football team that adorn our cottage overmantels. Mr. Gandish no doubt pointed out to his young gentlemen the importance of achieving, by means of a few simple technical devices, some sense of stability in pictorial composition.

134

Yet it is typical of Jung that in almost the same breath he lauds the virtues of the *'athanasius pharmakon'*, the medicament of immortality. Not that he commits himself to the certainty of immortality; like the idea of God, the idea of immortality is for Jung a functional utility, an archetypical product to be exploited for its psycho-therapeutic solace. He is in no way daunted by the draw-backs of borrowing from oriental dogmas and blending the product with ideas more appropriate to the demands of a western clientèle. One would have supposed that each of the variations on the theme of immortality would call for distinct systems of preparation for death. To those Eastern minds for whom death offers the refuge of personal extinction, a 'hygienic striving' for death may appear entirely logical; yet it is absurd to recommend it to Christians whose preparations are based on the assumption of a future life somewhat overshadowed by the fear of damnation. Jung's Western patients do not share the Oriental dread of *not* dying, knowing very well that they will die sooner than they like without trying. Nor are they goaded by a fear of waking up, e.g. in the form of a woman or as one of the minor coleoptera. The pious Buddhist's preparations for death are of the opposite sort from those of the pious Christian or pious Mahomedan. Jung cannot be denied the freedom to entertain a low opinion of the occidental's mental stamina; but his efforts to improve this alleged state of affairs by introducing oriental ideas into an occidental scheme leads to the postulation of a purely artificial Final Phase of Life. Moreover, as a professed agnostic Jung should have realized the danger of recom-

---

The need for stability gives rise to the demand for a *sense* of stability The psychological first-aid for the spectator provided by the artist in order to keep the former from feeling uncomfortable does not differ in principle from the mandala. Incidentally, if we may judge from the plates published in Jungian works, the latter-day mandalas designed by patients are dismal efforts reminiscent of *ye arte shoppe* and at times decorated with faces of a revolting silliness.

mending a fixed system of preparation for unspecified forms of immortality. For if one particular theory of immortality should happen to be correct, preparations for all other varieties must be not only a waste of good Third and/or Fourth Stage time, but positively detrimental to the individual's chances of salvation.

As for the more pretentious generalizations with which Jung punctuates his account of the problems of life and individuation, the best that can be said is that no doubt there are readers who derive a sense of uplift from them. It is of interest however that the more sweeping of these statements display the same slipshodness of thought that characterizes his theoretical formulations. The aphorism, that the person who does not say 'yes' to the power of the Destiny he finds within him cannot become an individual, is a case in point. Obviously if you can say 'no' to your destiny, the term has lost its meaning. Alternatively, if you *can* say 'no' to your destiny, you are just as much, possibly more, of a personality than he who says 'yes'. In either case you have established the superfluousness of Jungian 'individuation'. Why trouble to individuate in the face of destiny? Alternatively if destiny *is* the Self, why worry about innate destiny? Moreover if Jung's stages of life are accurately observed, man has at least four destinies. If his character is determined in the long run by eight distinct inherited tendencies he must have at least thirty-two possible destinies in a lifetime. Added to which the anima of men will multiply this total by two, the animi of women by 'n'. And what about the neuroses? If remediable neuroses can, as Jung suggests, function as signal-posts to individuation, why should not irremediable neuroses represent destinies in themselves?

Now it may be argued that when Jung talks of saying 'yes' to destiny, he means merely 'seizing a convenient opportunity', to which it can be returned, first, that if he does mean opportunity, he should say so, and, second, that even if he does mean opportunity, he is no better off. For who is to say that seizing an opportunity is inevitably the appropriate, desirable and adapted course of life? To the masochistic character-type neglect of opportunity or even renunciation may represent his destiny. Jung himself suggests that this is the case. Are we not told to put away childish and youthful things in the middle years of life and to renounce life itself during the fourth stage? If therefore we insist on saying 'yes' to life in its fourth stage, we are refusing to say 'yes' to our 'fourth stage destiny' which is death, and have therefore disqualified ourselves as individuated personalities. If however Jung really uses the term destiny in its accepted sense, the only plausible explanation of his equivocation is that, having invented the Collective Unconscious he can never get away from the idea of powerful and at the same time sacred innate tendencies existing in man. His concepts of destiny and of the self are merely repetitions of this essentially theological notion. The Collective Unconscious having been offered up on the altar of individuation, Destiny and the Self arise Phoenix-like from its ashes.

And here at long last we can come to grips with one of the main issues of the Freud-Jung controversy. Casual and ill-considered as it may appear, Jung's sweeping generalization regarding the relation of character to destiny is no happy-go-lucky Napoleonic improvisation. Not only does it reflect Jung's theoretical bias, it gives us also a reliable clue to his own attitude to life and its problems. By this one pronouncement he cuts the ground from under his claim to have given birth to a dynamic psychology that is at once creative and prospective. It is high time this myth was demolished. Ever since his renunciation of Freudian views, Jung has constantly attacked Freudian theories for their alleged neglect of the 'creative' aspects of mental life and for the stress they lay on the importance of infantile factors in the causation of mental conflict and illness. So violent is the Jungian objection

137

to the 'reductive' methods of psycho-analysis that one might almost imagine Freud was responsible for inventing the idea of cause and effect. On the other hand the stress laid by Jung on the prospective and creative function of the Collective Unconscious, on its 'spiritual' aspects and on its enriching and broadening influence on consciousness, reinforced of course by the vague language of 'uplift' in which he clothes his presentation, has led not only Jung's own disciples but an artless public to regard him as an apostle of self-realization, a profound and optimistic believer in the progressive evolution of the race.

Nothing could be further from the truth. A more pessimistic and nihilistic *Weltanschauung* than that presented by Jung in the form of a psychological theory could scarcely be conceived. It is rigid, mechanical and devoid of a spark of imagination; and it preaches a Jungian variety of predestination compared with which the psychic determinism of Freud can be regarded as sheer, soaring optimism. We are born, according to Jung, with tendencies that govern or should govern our whole development from the cradle to the grave. Behind the smiling mask of 'compensation' is hidden the grinning face of automatic reversal, which controls our emotions, our intelligence and our characteristic behaviour. Even our conflicts are stripped of every shred of human dignity: either they are due to onrushes of an unconscious constitutional factor or result from childish derelictions of a conscious 'duty' the origin of which is wrapped in mystery. Our stages of life are mapped out with a barrack-room indifference to individual development and human character which on closer examination can be traced to an absurd concern with alchemical values and numbers. The life-force chases its own tail round a rigidly closed 'psychic system'. It is incapable of any radical or permanent alteration during the lifetime of the individual: at most it can effect a minute change in the constitutional inheritance. We cannot even begin to 'individuate' until at the most conservative computation half of our life span is passed. And we must squander our last years preparing or at least pretending to prepare for a death that can only be made palatable by cultivating a therapeutic belief in the value of the *idea* of immortality.

Where in all this scheme is there a glimmer of hope for the progressive mental evolution of the race? Of the most malleable stages of life we are told next to nothing. Indeed one cannot but suspect that Jung knows next to nothing of the mental development of children. A moment's consideration should have shewn him that if changes can be wrought in the psychic organization of man, the necessary measures must be applied during these early labile stages of life when instinctual energies are capable of some degree of effective modification. If this cannot be achieved in infancy and early childhood, it certainly cannot be achieved through genteel individuations of adults approaching the climacteric. To his contempt for the neurotic Jung adds a condescending neglect of the mental achievements of childhood which is positively staggering in its naiveté. By the end of the first five years of life the child has weathered internal storms of love and hate; sustained profound hurts and deep disappointments; accommodated himself to an environment which is not only painfully inadequate to his hopes and fears but which, with the best or worst of intentions, may have behaved stupidly, even brutally to him. Despite these difficulties he has overcome to a large extent his boundless fears, has throttled down large charges of primitive and unteachable instinct and has directed large quantities to new goals. *Moreover—and this is perhaps the most remarkable of human achievements—he has succeeded in splitting some of his more primitive energies and has converted them into a more or less neutral form in which they can with reasonable luck be diverted towards more adapted aims.* These are achievements of which the average adult is totally incapable. They are achievements to which Jung, lost in academic and alchemical contemplation of adult man, has succeeded in remaining totally blind. Needless to add, the myth of a

139

spiritually creative Jungian psychology depends on the sedulous cultivation of yet another myth, which Jung and his followers are at pains to foster, namely, that Freudian psychology is a shortsighted, sterile and tendentious system based on a misapprehension of the facts of child life. Whereas if anything is obvious about mental life it is that only by taking an accurate measure of the disorders of child development can we ever hope to discover the point at which profound psychic changes can be effected. Freud at any rate leaves man with some vestige of hope that his archaic unreason may some day be modified or more effectively controlled. Jung leaves us without a vestige of hope. His *meaning* of life is a negation. The answer to the 'universal problem' is—nothing.

CHAPTER VIII

SOCIOLOGY, POLITICS AND ALCHEMY

IT is in accordance with the traditions of political and religious liberty that no man should suffer restriction of his
freedom of thought and speech because of his professional
activities. To be sure, the clergyman is generally expected to
set his own particular flock a good example by practising
whatever behaviouristic precepts he may happen to preach.
But this unwritten law is rarely regarded as unconscion-
able. The position of the psychologist in this matter is both
uneasy and uncertain, a state of affairs for which he is himself partly responsible. Being in the habit of laying down the
law on questions of motive, conscience and behaviour, he
cannot expect to be exempt from comment on the oft times
banality of his everyday judgements or the fallibility of his
conduct of practical affairs. It is only natural, for example,
that parents who have smarted under professional criticism
of their ways of bringing up their children should exhibit
some curiosity as to the outcome of the psychologist's efforts
to bring up his own offspring, and a certain malicious satis-
faction at his not infrequent failure.

As a matter of public interest, this issue is capable of
simple solution. It turns on the nature of the psycho-
therapeutic methods (if any) advocated by the psychologist.
Whoever ventures to teach or guide his patient has, whether
he knows it or not, usurped the privileges of the minister of
religion. He has laid claim to a form of infallibility which
in the case of the clergyman is justified only by the belief
that he is God's instrument. Attempts on the part of the
psycho-therapeutic persuasionist to escape this responsibility
by maintaining that he is concerned only with encouraging
'better' adaptations avail him little, for they imply that he
knows better than his patient what is 'good' for him and
ultimately that he is conversant with absolute norms of
function.

All of which is preamble to the statement that whereas the workaday psycho-therapeutist who is concerned with the alleviation or cure of mental disorders is entitled outside working hours to be as stupid as anyone else, this privilege cannot be accorded those who not only seek to direct their patients' lives but preach a quasi-theological brand of psychological conduct. In such instances the public is entitled to exhibit some curiosity as to the social, political and religious views of the psycho-therapeutist. When, as in the case of Jung, we are expressly informed that mental disorders are the result of a failure to perform a 'life-task,' that the main problem of life is one of 'individuation', and that this state can be achieved with the help of Jungian ministrations, we are surely entitled to examine his public and professional utterances for some indication of its ultimate form, or at least for some signposts to the way we should follow. If this should appear an unjustifiable procedure, it can only be said in extenuation that Jung has in any case invited scrutiny of his *Weltanschauung*. 'Higher Consciousness', he tells us, 'determines *Weltanschauung*. All consciousness of motives and intentions is germinating *Weltanschauung*. . . . He whose sun still revolves around the earth is a different person from him whose earth is the satellite of the sun'. Let us therefore sample the Jungian *Weltanschauung*.

SOCIOLOGY, POLITICS AND ALCHEMY. It is appropriate, as well as convenient, to consider Jung's sociological views in conjunction with his political opinions. Sociology can be defined as the pure science of group psychology; politics the applied science of group relations. Both, however, are intimately bound up with the psychology of the individual. Indeed, to those observers who regard the so-called 'group mind' as a specialized department of the individual psyche, the phenomena of group psychology can be understood only if they are interpreted in terms of individual development.

142

Freud, for example, regarded group psychology as being older than individual psychology: from the primal group or horde sprang the first individual, the primal father: the overthrow of the horde system and the relative composition of sexual rivalry through the medium of the family, gave an enormous impetus to the development of individual psychology. But the mechanisms of the group continued to display their primitive origin and content which can be conveniently studied, not only in the organization of primitive and civilized groups, but in the stages of development passed through by every infant on his road from infancy to that period of weaning from the family which begins at puberty.

Those who reject these hypotheses, holding that sociological phenomena are *sui generis* and based on special group instincts, are still bound to admit that the relation between politics and individual psychology is extremely close. For although politics are concerned very largely with the practical ordering of group relations, yet at every point in the social system the relation of 'individual expansion' to 'group order' raises the most acute political feeling. For this reason alone it would be justifiable to regard political systems as a form of applied group sociology, the principles of which have, however, been refracted through a medium of individual prejudice, bias, or in the rarest of instances, objective research. This goes far to explain why the average sociologist is a poor politician. The more politically minded he is the more he is at the mercy of emotional prejudice and consequently the more his views correspond with those of the man in the street. Sociological progress would, in fact, be infinitely more rapid if both laboratory and armchair sociologists were to illustrate their theoretical views with an account of their own political orientations and opinions. All of which leads to the conclusion that the best way of estimating the value of Jung's group psychology is to correlate it with such political opinions and prognostications as he has had the temerity to divulge.

143

To understand Jung's sociological values it is necessary however to interpolate here a brief reference to those parallels to the Jungian process of individuation which he finds in medieval Hermetic philosophy or *alchemy*, as well as in the various forms of Yoga. To alchemy he was apparently drawn by the similarity of the image patterns, dreams and visions supposedly produced by the Collective Unconscious on the one hand and by alchemic symbolism on the other. In his view medieval chemical experimentations were symbolic in nature; 'psychic processes expressed in pseudo-chemical language'. Trying to explain the nature of matter, the alchemist 'projected the unconscious into the darkness of matter, to illuminate it'. The *meditatio* of the alchemist is identical with the 'inner dialogue' by means of which alone man can come to terms with the Jungian Collective Unconscious. Similarly the alchemic philosophers had anticipated 'the problem of opposites as Analytical Psychology conceives it'. In their search for the philosopher's stone which would transmute the baser substances into gold, they projected into matter 'the mystery of psychic transformation' which leads to and at the same time is derived from the discovery of the transcendent Self. The divine demon, the God-man, the pneuma which enter (are projected) into matter 'stand for an unconscious component of the personality to which one might attribute a higher form of consciousness as well as *a superiority to common humanity*' (author's italics).

At a first glance all this may appear to have little to do with sociology. If Jung should regard alchemy as 'a halting step towards the most modern psychology' and find in its spontaneous, syncretized projections confirmation of the universal validity of the Jungian system, that, it may be argued, is his own funeral. Obviously, if the Jungian system can be deduced from the mental tendencies and systems of the alchemist, alchemical tendencies and systems are just as likely to be found in the Jungian system; witness, for example, Jung's view that 'a perception of the significance of fourness . . . means illumination of the "inner region" . . . a first step, a necessary station on the road of individual development'. The flaw in the Jungian correlation is due to the fact that, having rejected the Freudian unconscious system, Jung has deprived himself of the concept of unconscious *defence mechanisms* whose functions it is not only to restrain primitive instinctual forces but *to conceal the workings of the unconscious mind*. The Collective Unconscious which Jung offers us in place of the Freudian unconscious contains no defence mechanisms. Its expressions must always be regarded as 'positive' manifestations. The Jungian archetype is always a positive, unmodified expression of an inherited collective tendency. The unconscious symbol of Freud, it is true, allows a marginal expression of unconscious forces; but it functions also as an effective *disguise* of (defence against) unconscious content. Even if we assume that alchemy is a primitive form of unconscious psychology, we have no reason to suppose that the psychological system it represents is a valid one: on the contrary, it is safe to assume that it conceals unconscious psychic function much more than it expresses it. Jung's attempt to tie up his psychology with earlier alchemical forms of thought was a disastrous blunder: it inevitably laid the Jungian system open to the criticism that *it conceals the true nature of mind much more than it illuminates it*. And this, as we have seen, is an extremely charitable estimate of its validity.

But to return to sociology: the most significant of Jung's correlations between his own psychological system and the system of alchemical philosophy lies in the idea of *redemption*. In his view the 'secret' sought after by the alchemist by which base metal could be transmuted into noble substance, represents the need to transform the personality 'through the mixing of and forming of noble and base constituents, of the undifferentiated and inferior function, of the conscious and the (collective) unconscious'. In fact, the Jungian processes of individuation and transformation. Here Jung begins to propound an (alchemical) sociology. The modern

145

projection of the alchemical problem of the opposites is, he says, represented by collectivity and the individual; or, society and personality. 'For it seems as if the building up of collective life and the unprecedented massing together of man, so characteristic of our time, were needed to make the individual aware of the fact that he was being strangled in the meshes of the organized mob.' The First World War, Jung maintains, arose because European man was possessed by something that robbed him of free choice. Change of this state 'can begin only with individuals, since masses—as we know only too well—are blind beasts'.

At this point the disillusioned sociologist who has made a study of the various forms of *Führer-prinzip* will no doubt begin to smell a rat. For if the redemption of the individual involves, as Jung says it does, his isolation from the masses, it will not be long before we find that true Jungian individuation not only implies the possession of God-like or Christ-like qualities, but sets its owner above the law. The term 'individual', it may be surmised, will turn out to be synonymous with 'leader'. Now it will be remembered that spontaneous individuation is, according to Jung, to be found only amongst our rarer spirits. And although at one or two points he qualifies this statement by saying that vocation, which as we have seen is equivalent to inner destiny, 'also belongs to the small ones all the way down to the duodecimo format', he qualifies this qualification by adding that on the way down it becomes more veiled and unconscious, till it finally merges into one with society, surrendering its own wholeness to social convention and conventional necessity. Indeed, as Jung himself remarks, many are called but few are chosen. 'Only the few', he goes on, 'have hit upon this strange adventure (of developing personality).' They are as a rule 'the legendary heroes of mankind'. They are likewise liberated from convention. Their vocation 'acts like a law of God from which there is no escape'. *They must obey their own law.*' 'They thrust themselves up like mountain peaks out of the mass that clings to its collective fears, connexions, laws and methods, and chose their own way.' The inner voice of these personalities, however, brings to consciousness whatever the whole nation or humanity suffers from. 'But it presents this evil in individual form . . . in a temptingly convincing way . . . if we do not succumb to it in part then nothing of this evil goes into us, and then also no renewal and no healing can take place.' If the 'I' completely succumbs to the inner voice, its contents act as if they were so many devils. But if the 'I' succumbs only in part and saves itself by self-assertion from being swallowed, 'it is seen that the evil is only an evil semblance'. The road to leadership, it would seem, is beset with inner dangers.

Apparently emboldened by his own formulations, Jung marches with confidence on to the thin ice of political generalization and prognostication. First of all, he expresses his democratic faith: 'As a Swiss I am an inveterate democrat, yet I recognize that nature is aristocratic, and, what is more, esoteric'.[1] Having so shriven himself, he then goes on: 'the great liberating deeds of world history have come from leading personalities and never from the inert mass that is secondary at all times and needs the demagogue if it is to move at all'. 'The pæan of the Italian nation', he adds, 'is addressed to the personality of the Duce, and the dirges of other nations lament the absence of great leaders.' Lest we should be in doubt as to the nature of great leaders, Jung adds a footnote which should be quoted in full. It runs: '*This chapter was originally given as lecture entitled* Die Stimme des Innern *at the Kulturbund, Vienna, in November* 1932. *Since then Germany too has found its leader*'.

That this footnote was more than an impersonal comment is borne out by a number of circumstances. When criticized by Dr. G. Bally for becoming editor of the Nazified *Zentralblatt für Psychotherapie*, Jung maintained that by taking this step he had exposed himself to misunderstanding 'which no one can escape who, out of a higher necessity, has

[1] Compare Hitler in *Mein Kampf:* '. . . the parliamentary principle of the majority sins against the basic aristocratic principle in nature'.

to come to terms with the powers that be in Germany'.[1]
'The sciences, the art of healing and every other art . . .
must learn to adapt themselves. To protest is ridiculous!'

In 1936, developing his 'psycho-political analysis' in
terms of the aristocratic tendency in nature, Jung states
specifically 'Communistic or Socialistic democracy is an upheaval of the unfit against attempts at order'. And again:
'The S.S. men are being transformed into a caste of knights
ruling sixty million natives'. 'There are two types of dictators, the chieftian type and the Medicine-man type.
Hitler is the latter. He is the mouthpiece of the gods of old
. . . the Sibyl . . . the Delphic oracle'. Early in 1939 he
advises the Western statesmen 'not to touch Germany in her
present mood. She is much too dangerous. . . . Let her go
into Russia. There is plenty of land there—one-sixth of the
surface of the earth'.[2] And again, in his essay on Wotan:
'The worshippers of Wotan, in spite of their eccentricity
and crankiness, seemed to have judged the empirical facts
more correctly than the worshippers of reason'. Referring
to events in Germany during 1936, he maintains that although Wotan has shown himself as 'restless, violent and
stormy', his 'ecstatic and prophetic qualities' will become
manifest 'in the course of the next years or decades';
'National Socialism would not be the last word'; its destiny
would be one 'which perhaps none but the seer, the prophet,
the Fuhrer himself can foretell . . .' 'The true leader is
always led (by his unconscious). We can see it at work in
him. He himself (Hitler) has referred to his Voice'.

Needless to say, these indications of Jung's political
orientation and sagacity are embedded in a mass of generalizations from which the contrary impression might appear
that his concern had always been with the dæmonic
(reactionary) aspects of any group expression of that Collective Unconscious without which, we had been told in the
same breath, no progress can be made in any direction.

[1] *Neue Zürcher Zeitung*, 13 March 1934.
[2] *Cosmopolitan* interview, January 1939.

After the event, Jung was as wise as any other political pundit who has perpetrated a howler. He had apparently known what was going to happen all the time; had deduced it in fact as early as 1918, when, analysing German patients, he had observed '*specifically* German archetypes' the emergence of which spelled disaster. The 'blonde beast', he had said then, was stirring and apocalyptic events were afoot. After the defeat of Germany in 1945 his picture of Hitler underwent a remarkable transformation. The hermaphroditic figure of the 'religious' medicine-man *cum* Sibyl, the 'demi-deity' presented to us in 1936 had given place to that of a 'psychic scarecrow (with a broomstick for his outstretched arm)', a hysteric, suffering from *pseudologia phantastica*, a psychopath leading his millions to a mass-psychosis, which incidentally was no longer, as once in Jung's eyes, a manifestation peculiar to the U.S.S.R. Germany had been and still was psychically ill, although, to be sure, the illness was one prevalent throughout Europe. 'The psychologist cannot make a distinction between the mentality of the Nazis and of the regime's opponents.' The great archetype, Wotan, had, it would seem, left the German like a 'drunkard awakening with a hangover'.

Under ordinary circumstances it would be only decent to allow the political *gaffes* of professional psychologists to sink into oblivion. This is in any case a privilege demanded by and often accorded practising politicians. Had Jung's political views been purely personal we could well dismiss them with the comment that by the grace of God and the rapid passage of military events, he was just saved from covering himself with everlasting ridicule. As we have seen, however, Jung's claims to foresight and his doctrine of individuation deprive him of this privilege. What is perhaps more important, it would appear that this particular brand of thinking passes as scientific amongst members of the educated public who ought by now to know better. Mr. Kingsley Martin, who, though no doubt a mild authoritarian *in posse*, could not by the wildest stretch of the imagination be called a pro-Nazi, tells us[1] that although he is far yet from grasping or being able to appraise Jung's theory of the human mind, he finds Jung 'the most exciting and encouraging of living writers'. Apparently oblivious to the fact that if you accept the Jungian theory of the Collective Unconscious and with it, of course, the Jungian theory of individuation, you have committed yourself to some form of *Führer-prinzip*, he welcomes Jung's explanations of mass reactions, regarding them, indeed, as having 'a moral not only for Germany'. This being the case we may fairly proceed to examine the scientific status of the new Jungian sociology.

The reader will no doubt recall that the Jungian Collective Unconscious, which operating somehow with an undifferentiated *élan vital* (the Jungian libido) is responsible ultimately for both Good and Evil, for the reactionary dæmonic in as well as the God-like Vocation of Man, represents a legacy of inherited tendencies dating, according to taste, from the first emergence of the unicellular organism, from the dawn of primitive culture or from the post-Reformation period. And he may have surmised that, if this be the case, the influence of the Collective Unconscious must be remarkably selective as well as remarkably unselective. So he will not be altogether surprised to note that Jung not only subscribes to an aristocratic theory of nature but has cultivated a special brand of racial theory. Let us again consult 'Wotan', an essay published by Jung in the same month of 1936 in which Hitler reoccupied the Rhineland. Why, Jung asks, should Wotan, the old God of storm and frenzy, awake in a civilized country, giving rise to the *Jugendbewegung*, to the marching unemployed hordes of the Weimar republic; why, when 'the Hitler movement brought the whole of Germany to its feet' should he produce 'the spectacle of a great migration of people marking time'. Jung answers his question with an explanation of

[1] *New Statesman*, 11 September 1948.

the nature of National Socialism: 'Wotan the wanderer was awake'. In other words, the *furor teutonicus*. 'Wotan represents a primeval Germanic factor and . . ., is the most accurate expression and inimitable personification of a basic human quality which is particularly characteristic of the German . . . '; a God has 'taken possession' of the Germans and their house is filled with 'a mighty wind'. 'Could we', Jung asks elsewhere[1] 'conceive of anyone but a German writing *Faust* or *Also Sprach Zarathustra?*' Both play upon something that reverberates in the German soul—a 'primordial image . . . the figure of a physician or teacher of mankind'. Already in 1927[2] he had maintained that 'Wotan and not the God of the Christians is the God of the Germans'. If there be any doubt as to the nature of this side of Jung's racial theory, consider his comment on Hitler's 'religion'.[3] 'Like Mohammedanism, it teaches the virtue of the sword . . . Hitler's first idea is to make his people powerful because the spirit of the Aryan German deserves to be supported by might, muscle and steel.'

But this was by no means Jung's first essay in the theory of racial characteristics and superiorities. Already in 1914 Freud had commented on Jung's 'racial prejudices'. These appeared to be focused in the first instance on psychological theories; witness Jung's statement that 'it could be an unpardonable mistake to accept the conclusions of a Jewish psychology as generally valid'. The racial angle was even more pointed in Jung's editorial Foreword to the first number of the Nazified[4] *Zentralblatt für Psychotherapie*, where he laid down that the new policy of the Journal would be to differentiate between Germanic and Jewish psychologies:

[1] *Modern Man in Search of a Soul.*
[2] *Der Leuchter*, 1927.
[3] *Cosmopolitan* interview, 'Diagnosing the Dictators', January 1939.
[4] This contained also a pronouncement by Professor Dr. jur. Dr. med. M.H. Goering that members of the German Medical Association for Psychotherapy are expected 'to have made a serious scientific study of Adolf Hitler's fundamental book *Mien Kampf* and to recognize it as a basic work'.

' . . . the definite distinctions between Germanic and Jewish psychology long apparent to sensible people shall no longer be obscured'. In the second number Jung continues: ' . . . the *Aryan unconscious* (author's italics), however, contains buoyancy, creative germs of a future yet to be realized, which one cannot depreciate as romance of the nursery, without becoming mentally endangered'. And again, 'The Aryan unconscious has a higher potentiality than the Jewish'. Medical psychology, he goes on, has committed the grave error of applying Jewish categories blindly to Christian Germans and Slavs. 'My warning voice was suspected of anti-semitism for decades. This suspicion originated with Freud. He had no knowledge of the Germanic soul—just as little as all his German parrots. Has the amazing phenomenon of National Socialism at which the whole world looks with astounded eyes taught them better?' The force that gave rise to National Socialism 'lay hidden in the Germanic soul, in that deep ground which is anything but the garbage-pail of unfulfillable childhood wishes . . . '; and yet again, 'I put the Jewish question on the table of the house. I have done this deliberately . . . the Jewish problem is a complex, a festering wound . . . '

To judge the 'scientific' nature of these racial theories, we must read them in conjunction with his theory of 'Earth Conditioning of the Psyche'.[1] Jung regarded the settlement of the North American continent by a predominantly Germanic population as 'the greatest experiment' in race-transplantation. In the second generation a 'Yankee type' is formed 'so similar to the Indian type' that one would have immediately attributed it to miscegenation, had one not known that there was only an infinitesimal mixture of Indian blood in the North American. The mysterious Indian-izing of the American population only became clear to Jung when he treated analytically a great number of Americans. The next thing that struck him was the great influence of the Negro—'psychological influence, of course'. The lively

[1] *Der Leuchter*, 1927.

temperament of the American at baseball games 'can hardly be derived from the Germanic forbears; it is rather to be likened to the "chattering" of the Negro village'. And so to the conclusion: 'Thus, the American presents to us a strange picture: a European with Negro mannerisms and an Indian soul'. In the air and soil of a country there is 'an x and a y which slowly permeate man and mould him to the type of the aboriginal inhabitant . . . ' 'I remember particularly seeing in New York a family of German immigrants. Three of the children had been born in Germany and four in America. The first three were clearly Germans, whilst the others were unmistakably Americans'. So apparently the Collective Unconscious is not after all the final determinant of human character and behaviour. The x and y of air and soil, it would seem, can do more in a couple of generations than the Collective Unconscious can do in a million years. But not, singularly enough, to Jews. Generations of residence in Switzerland, Germany, Czechoslovakia, Poland, the Americas and the Antipodes leave their archetypes severely unaltered. No moulding to the aboriginal type takes place. Indeed when Jews produce psychologies they are, of their archetypical and projective nature, purely Jewish. The German, it is to be presumed, despite his climatic pliability, still clings to the archetypical Wotan wherever he is born. Yet the psychologist is warned not to make a distinction between the mentality of the Nazis, a Wotan-determined characteristic, and the mentality of their opponents. Further comment is needless.

CHAPTER IX

RELIGION

RELIGION. But if Jung's sociology and politics, despite their manifest shoddiness and shallowness, secure some degree of acceptance amongst intellectuals, it is not surprising to find that, his modest demurs notwithstanding, Jung is often hailed as a great religious teacher. To be sure, the otherwise enthusiastic Priestley is cautious enough to qualify his encomiums by saying that Jung comes 'near' to religion. As will be seen, by this cautious use of the preposition, any variety of heretical belief can be described as 'religious'. But however cautious devotees to Jung may be, much less discretion is exhibited by accredited Jungian practitioners. Dr. G. Adler claims that the religious outlook 'regained' by Jung is 'a fundamentally new step in human consciousness'. Jacobi goes even further, stating categorically that 'Jung leads the patient to an experience of God in his own breast', and that even unbelievers 'will be led through the experience of the "inward God" in themselves to Him'. Small wonder that even such an acute and dexterous theologian as Dean Inge, though ready to admit that Jung is not a 'convinced believer', should nevertheless charge Freud with producing a 'psychology without a psyche' and maintain that 'his rival Jung is wiser, since he sees clearly that religious faith is a cure in many neurotic cases.'[1]

The reader seeking for evidence of Jung's 'religious' or 'near religious' outlook will be well advised to take with him some etymological definitions of 'religion' and of 'numinosity'; and he may reasonably accept the standard derivation according to which religion is a belief in and reverence for the Gods, and the numinous means divine will, power and majesty. Jung's own definition runs: religion is 'a care-

[1] In an 'Introduction' to *The Dangers of Being Human*, by Edward Glover (Allen & Unwin).

ful and scrupulous observation of . . . the *Numinosum*, that is, a dynamic existence or effect not caused by an arbitrary act of will'. To this is added by Jung and his followers a variety of supplementary definitions. Thus, the religious process is simply the process of individuation: it is a ritualistic process performed for the purpose of producing at will the effect of the *numinosum*, a belief in an objective divine cause always preceding: it is the attitude of a consciousness which has been altered by experience of the *numinosum*.

Jung's list of the objects of religion includes besides Gods, spirits, etc., a number of abstractions 'laws, ideas, ideals' . . . anything worthy of adoration or love. 'The human soul seems to harbour mysteries, since to an empiricist all religion boils down to a peculiar condition of the mind' . . . 'One could even define *religious experience* as that kind of experience which is *characterized by the highest appreciation* (author's italics) no matter what the contents are. Modern mentality . . . will turn to the soul as a last hope.' This hope however, appears to be beyond consciousness: we 'must admit that the unconscious is at times capable of assuming an intelligence and purposivness superior to actual conscious insight'. There is little doubt, says Jung, that this fact is a 'basic religious phenomenon'. 'The non-ego has all the quality of "eternity" or of relative timelessness.' The unconscious, we may remember, is also, according to Jung, 'an almost immortal human being', a psychic process or activity that is to say, infinite, near eternal and almost unchangeable.

Clearly then we must seek for the Jungian God in the first place in the Jungian Collective Unconscious. The difficulty is to establish which of the various derivatives or parts of the Collective Unconscious qualifies for apotheosis. Sometimes it appears to be the Collective Unconscious as a whole; but this view is offset by another according to which one of the focal points or 'personalities' of the impersonal unconscious, the Shadow, can function as the Devil. Presumably then God must exist in some other part. This is no difficulty

to Jung, who regards the Christian Trinity as being a muti-
lated Quarternity from which the Devil has been arbitrarily
shorn. And the Quaternity, it should be explained, is nothing
more than the alchemical formula of the Jungian Collective
Unconscious. Even the Jungian mandala, the symbolic figure
of individuation, has acquired a religious connotation: it
signifies either 'the hitherto dormant divine being, now
extracted and revivified'; or it symbolizes 'the vessel or room
in which the transformation of man into a divine being
takes place'. Lastly, the *élan vital* (Jungian Libido) falls
under suspicion. 'We might be tempted by modern philosophy to call energy or the *élan vital* God.' But this is apparently not practical psychology. 'Whether energy is God or
God is energy, concerns one very little . . . but to give *appropriate* psychological explanation—this I must be able to do.'

On the whole two main tendencies appear to emerge from
this multiplicity of definitions: one, that the *idea* of God is a
Collective archetype, the other that religion is an *experience*
of the individuated Self, which, it may be remembered, combines both unconscious and conscious attitudes to life. A
third possibility exists, namely, that God and the Self combine in an archetype.   Dr. Adler, for example, states: 'The
archetype of the Deity in the human psyche, Jung has
termed the "Self". ' 'The experience of the non-ego', says
Adler in this connexion, 'is perceived as "God".' It is important to note, however, that the *archetypical image of the
Deity is not meant to prove the existence of God*, only the
existence of the archetype 'which', says Jung, 'to my mind
is the most we can say psychologically about God'. The Ego
is 'subordinated to, or contained in, a superordinated Self
as a centre of the Total, Illimitable and Indefinable psychic
personality'. 'All that psychology can legitimately do is to
. . . accept the possibility that "God within us" corresponds
to a transcendental reality.' The 'God without' must apparently shift for himself. Expressing some of these notions in
terms of the psycho-therapy of the neuroses Jung remarks
'If a psycho-neurosis must be understood as the suffering of

a human being who has not discovered what life means for him, then the discovery of the eternal images of meaning and significance as most intensely expressed in the experience of the "Self" as the Archetype of the Deity, indeed means a cure'. Accused of 'casting out devils by Beelzebub, an honest neurosis by the cheat of a religious belief,' Jung replies 'there is no question of *belief*, but of *experience* which is absolute. *Is there any better truth about ultimate things than the one that helps you to live?*' (author's italics.) To the Jungian pantheon of endopsychic Gods are hereby added environmental experience and such specific therapeutic agents as alcohol, tea and aspirin.

Remembering the official Christian definition of God as a 'spirit, infinite, eternal and unchangeable', we may well inquire at this point as to the theological status of the Jungian soul and spirit of man, the *anima(-us-i)*. The answer is that for purposes of religious discussion, it loses its earlier structural and functional connotations and becomes a vague caption which the casual reader might well take to mean the spirit of God. 'We moderns' must rediscover 'the life of the spirit' and 'experience it anew for ourselves'. There is a 'world of the spirit whose active principle is . . . "God".' This spirit, incidentally, 'to ensure its own existence, must often deny and overcome an obtrusive, physical fact'. Past ages, Jung observes, held the individual soul to be dependent upon a World System of the Spirit, viz., God. 'Certainly a near eternal (sic) being may appropriately (sic) be called divine.' So, after all, the anima appears to be identical either with the 'near-eternal' Collective Unconscious or with the total psyche, ego-consciousness excluded. Yet even ego-consciousness is included in the Jungian total psyche. So the anima in its religious sense may mean anything, everything or nothing. This is remote indeed from Jung's clinical definitions of the 'soul' as either the personality, or 'a definitely demarcated function-complex', or again man's unconscious attitude to the Collective Unconscious, or a focal personality of the unconscious, or a set of archetypes or the contra-

sexual. As has been emphasized to the point of tedium, Jung
has little or no regard for the meaning of meaning. Like the
idea of God, a definition is for him a functional utility of
man, to be used 'appropriately'. Since all psychic processes,
whether transcendental or instinctual in origin, are according to Jung, energy in motion, no contradiction exists for
him between a 'function-complex' and the 'idea of God'.
Indeed, despite his assertion that it is immaterial to man
whether God is energy or energy God, one is left with the
impression that Jung believes the true God to be *élan vital*.
In this respect he differs only in the choice of 'archetype'
from the worshippers of Priapus.

We are now in a position to outline the Jungian theology.
In the beginning was the psychic fact. Ideas are facts. An
idea occurring in an individual is subjective but, according
to Jung, becomes objective when it is established by society
—a *consensus gentium*. In any case, certain ideas 'create
themselves almost everywhere'. They exist in the Collective
Unconscious, exercise autonomous power and can apparently
interfere with the life of man like an autonomous being.
Psychic happenings constitute our only immediate experience. Some are derived from material environment, others
seem to come from a mental source. 'Whether I picture to
myself the car I wish to buy or try to imagine the state in
which the soul of my dead father now is . . . both happenings
are psychic reality.' This reality can, however, be transformed and falsified by the psyche. The psyche is an 'incomprehensible something'. Even our instincts 'are con-
tinually colliding with something and why should not this
something be called spirit?'

Whether this something be spirit, or an archetype of the
Deity or a transcendental self that has accepted the psychic
facts of the Collective Unconscious, experience of it is numinous and potentially dangerous. It may be experienced as a
feeling or as a voice or observed as a mandala and, provided
its dangers are overcome, can give rise to religious ecstasy.
Our naive ancestors projected their unconscious contents,

158

good or bad, light or dark, into matter. By so doing they sought at the same time to avoid the dangers of unconscious 'experience' and to find 'the meaning of life' in the external world. This, thinks Jung, is no longer necessary or indeed quite possible. The alchemical number '4', for example, now proves to be 'an archetype of extraordinary significance for the psyche'. It gives the pure spirit its 'bodiliness'. 'We have, at last, to admit that the tetrakys is something psychical . . . An idea of God, utterly absent from the mind of modern man, returns in a form used consciously 300–400 years ago.' The dangers of 'immediate experience', which appear to be reminiscent of the dangers of seeing Jehovah face to face, can be neutralized by ritual. Indeed the function of 'so-called religion', i.e., Dogma or Ritual, is to protect against 'further immediate experience'. In this respect Catholics are better off than Protestants. 'I support the hypothesis of the practising Catholic *while it works for him*' (author's italics) as a defence against grave risk (of immediate experience presumably) without asking 'the academic question whether the defence is more or less true'. Yet, according to Jung, Dogmas began life as a 'revealed' immediate experience. In brief Christian dogmas are or were archetypical.

As regards the meaning of life, Jung continues to wobble. At one time it was the process of individuation; but in its theological aspect it becomes the 'vast psychic background whose nature . . . (the ego) . . . may apprehend, but which it has in no sense created'. This is now seen to contain 'the real meaning of existence' . . . 'It explains the stupendous nature of all visions of God.' And it explains the dangers of immediate experience; the unguarded ego may be over-come by these visions and retreat into a psychosis. In short, we are left with the impression that the Jungian *idea* of God is a *two-way system* manifested, in reversible order, in the Total Psyche, in the Collective Unconscious, in certain Archetypes including the number 4, in the Anima (but not, of course, the Shadow), in Numinous Experience, in the Self, originally but not latterly in Dogma, in any form of

159

Appreciation, in anything that Helps Us To Live, and in the *Élan Vital.*

It would serve no useful purpose to examine this system in detail. It is perhaps sufficient to say that it is founded on a false premise regarding the nature of psychic reality. Jung is never tired of emphasizing that a psychic event is an event; but he does not care to add that a true notion differs from a false notion though both exist as psychic events. If we had stuck to the *consensus gentium* as a proof of objective reality, we would still believe that the earth is flat. Even Jung admits that the archetypical nature of the 'craving for God' does not guarantee its factual truth. To him this is no matter: it is archetypical. We are to be made happy in this respect by sucking our thumbs. Over and over again it is made perfectly clear that *the archetypical Idea of God has nothing to do with the absolute existence of God.* In any case the absolute existence or non-existence of God is not, according to Jung, the psychologist's business.   Having excluded God, and thereby *presumably* the supernatural in general, from the consideration of the psychologist, he proceeds to invest *human* ideas and images with an atmosphere politely described as mysticism, but which the less polite observer would call an atmosphere of religiosity.   Jung cannot or will not see that however primary and archetypical the God-idea may be, it is *in itself* no more supernatural than the idea of a saucepan. Talk of the God within means nothing if the idea of God without is not objectively true. Jung cannot perhaps be expected to determine whether it is objectively true or not. But at any rate his fundamental evasion of the issue cuts the ground from under his pretensions to be a spiritual guide. If it is not the psychologist's business to investigate the objective truth of the existence of God, neither is it his business to build up a pseudo-religion out of primordial religious yearning and a multitude of myths. It is no reward to seekers after the 'meaning of life' to be

160

invited to fill their bellies with the East wind, and like it. They might just as reasonably be asked to worship *sal volatile*.

Finally it is to be noted that the Jungian theological system is intended not only for the use of patients, but also for the generality of mankind. Being a master of evasion he gives few direct hints as to the nature of his own religious beliefs or of that 'religious outlook' he is said to have 'regained' for humanity. And following his assumption that the actual existence of God is not the psychologist's business, he might well maintain that the nature of his own religious beliefs is nobody's business. This argument has already been examined and rejected. Whoever seeks to instruct his patients in mythological parallels and pre-religious superstitions, is under obligation to disclose his own convictions. Occasionally, however, Jung is indiscreet enough to give the interested reader a clue. He sometimes calls himself a Protestant, a position which would give him more play for his many inventions, numina and the like; it appears that the Protestant, being less protected by Dogma than the modern Catholic, and totally unprotected by the system of Catholic Confession, is more open to the numinous and potentially dangerous experience of the stupendous vision of the *idea* of God. At other times, however, Jung is seemingly a mere agnostic believing 'what he thinks he knows'.

Further evidence can only be inferred from Jung's various pronouncements. For example, he will never admit that a God is a *different thing* from an object of admiration. In fact there is no evidence that he believes either that there is a God or that there is a future life. The existence of the *idea* of God is an 'interesting' psychological fact; numinous experience, which appears to be little more than a narcissistic enjoyment of the religious sentiment, is also an 'interesting' psychic phenomenon. These ideas and interests are, however, like Guinness, good for us. And we are recommended to feel and behave as if there were an actual God and a future life. How we should accomplish this feat and what exactly we should feel is nowhere indicated. Whether his patients believe in the objective reality of God or are mere idolators or in the last resort are poor orphans of nothing, does not seem to matter to Jung in the slightest. 'Just as primitive man was able with the aid of religious and philosophical symbols to free himself from his original state, so the neurotic can shake off his illness.' Not that belief in religious or philosophical dogma is to be thrust upon the patient. He is simply to resume that *psychological attitude* which in an earlier civilization, was characterized by a living belief in religious or philosophical dogma. Not to put too fine a point on it, the 'religious outlook' Jung recommends is like a belief or rather a *pretended* belief in Santa Claus. Indeed, if Jung himself only *pretended* there *was* a God, one could more readily believe in the sincerity of his attempt to impose 'religious attitudes' on all and sundry. As it is, the effect of his theological exertions is to reduce his former ideas as to the nature of individuation to nothing. At one time individuation represented to him 'the meaning of life'. This, at any rate, was a positive though rather vague assertion. But since he got his ideas mixed up with setting suns and Indian customs, this has disappeared in a mist of quasi-theological generalities which when evaporated leaves no residue. We are, seemingly, all part of something. But unless he believes there is a *Something not Ourselves* that makes for Righteousness, this is, theologically regarded, a mere manner of speaking. For the rest we are left with the *numinosum*, a religious sentiment or affect aroused by the *idea* of God, which in turn is a legacy from our primordial ancestors, springing directly from an innate disposition. This numinosum, its potential dangers neutralized by Dogma or Individuation, is the final spiritual comfort Jung has to offer his battered and baffled fellow men.

No doubt it will be argued that Jung himself cannot be held responsible for the credulity of those followers who regard him as a great religious or near-religious teacher. They may point out that he has himself disclaimed any

162

intention of producing either a religious or a philosophic system. And in a formal sense both of these arguments are sound enough. For Jung is certainly no philosopher, still less a believer. No doubt, too, the increasing support given to Jungian psychology by clerics can be regarded less as a tribute to Jung's religiosity than as a reaction to Freud's view that religion is one of the illusions wherewith man seeks to soften the asperities of life and to stay the fundamental discontents engendered by civilization. It is all the more necessary therefore to point out what is apparently effectively concealed in a mass of Jungian verbiage, that so far from being religious in tendency, Jung's system is fundamentally irreligious. Nobody is to care whether God exists, Jung least of all. All that is necessary is to 'experience' an 'attitude' because it 'helps one to live'. Had Jung propounded this system in those Middle Ages, so dear to him because of their alchemical associations, he would certainly have been burned at the stake. Apparently, too, he followed in the footsteps of his alchemical forbears. For just as they projected their unconscious phantasies in the form of chemical researches into the nature of matter, so Jung has projected into modern psychology a bevy of bogus gods and goddesses masquerading as psychic concepts. If it be true that man gradually adds to the archetypical content of the Jungian Collective Unconscious, we may anticipate with some confidence that the Jungian system will some day acquire an archetypical *mana*. Perhaps it has already done so. For in addition to being a heretic, Jung is essentially an idolator who has created a multiplicity of gods within, and asks other people to enjoy the experience of thinking of them.

That the 'religious outlook' is not outwardly but inwardly directed towards the *archetypical idea* of God; that the Deity is the presumed unconscious attitude of our just-not-simian ancestors, preserved by a presumed process of just-not-quite ideational inheritance; and that 'spirit' is just a Jungian synonym for the Collective Unconscious may or may not trouble Jungians and Christians: it is exactly the

FREED OR JUNG

sort of thing that repelled the heathenish mind of Freud.
Writing of the infantile origins of religion and of the rear-
guard actions fought in favour of religious systems by those
who must see that they are not tenable, Freud interpolated
a comment which might well be pondered by those who
regard Jung as the founder of a new Near-Religion. 'One,
would like,' he wrote, 'to count oneself among the believers
so as to admonish the philosophers who try to preserve the
God of religion by substituting for him an impersonal
shadowy, abstract principle, and say "thou shalt not take
the name of the Lord, thy God, in vain!"'

CHAPTER X

ART

OF the artist's relations to the psychologist it can be said
with some justice that their cordiality is in inverse ratio to
their depth. From the professed conscious psychologist the
artist has nothing to hope and therefore little to fear. Inured
to the attentions of the qualified 'art critic', he can well
afford to treat with cheerful contempt the amateur efforts
of those academic psychologists whose researches have never
brought them within hailing distance of human motivation,
or at any rate much farther than a knowledge of the physiology of the sensory organs can carry them. The dynamic
psychologist who is familiar with unconscious mental function and motivation is in different case. Whether or not he
is competent to appraise artistic achievements he cannot
turn his back on those psychic products which not only
contribute so much to man's aesthetic feeling and thereby
to his enjoyment of life, but are capable of arousing the most
violent states of emotional rapport with or prejudice against
the artist.

Inevitably the psycho-analyst's prentice efforts to penetrate the mysteries of art were concentrated on the written
and spoken word. The number of psycho-analytical studies
of literature and folklore exceeds by far the number concerned with painting and sculpture; and significantly
enough psycho-analytical essays on the nature of music are
few and far between. Although no doubt this distribution
of interest is to some extent the result of a timidity arising
from technical ignorance, it is nevertheless an accurate
index of the tractability of the different materials to psycho-
analysis. Naturally the most accessible psychic products are
those conveyed through auditory or word-thinking. From
about the age of two and a half years the expression of
emotional stress through organised speech is reasonably

effective. By this time the (Freudian) pre-conscious system of the mind is comparatively well organised, and unconscious and conscious phantasy-formations develop rapidly. Hence the end-products of auditory thinking are perfectly capable of direct analysis. As the examination of the early play-drawings of infants has clearly demonstrated, analytic technique can also be applied to the products of visual thinking, although the conclusions drawn from early drawing, painting and modelling are by no means fool-proof. The influence on psychic development of earlier forms of sensory experience, i.e., of unmodified sound stimuli, of smell, taste and touch; the variations in muscular tension; and above all the recording of different quantities and qualities of rhythmic stimulation, through whichever sensory channel these may operate, have already been harnessed in the interests of psychic expression long before speaking, drawing and writing are available as mental instruments. Naturally therefore the arts of music, miming, dancing and the like retain a connection with primitive instinctual expression which is more direct and immediate than later artistic forms ; and, however elaborately they may be developed, they are less capable of accurate analysis than are those organised visual and auditory products (pictorial and verbal representations) which lend themselves to elaborate pre-conscious phantasy-activity. Nevertheless these earlier psychic forms constitute the foundations of infantile mental life and must consequently be regarded as being subject to the recognised laws that govern psychic affairs in general. If we cannot directly analyse these products, we must at least be able to make plausible reconstructions of their psychic content, aim and significance. And what more plausible than that they continue throughout life to give vent to the early hopes, fears and aspirations experienced by the embryonic mind of the infant, that they represent the first forms of magical expression, wherewith the infant strives to counter the primitive anxieties of life, love, hate and death, in other words to objectivate the whole paraphernalia of infantile conflict.

The fact that some forms of creative activity are incapable of direct psychological analysis and that their content can only be inferred serves to increase the gulf existing between the psycho-analyst and the writer on aesthetics. It is only exasperating to the latter to find that the highly sophisticated interpretations he is ready to offer of, for example, musical productions are regarded by the dynamic psychologist as purely (pre)-conscious in origin, still more annoying to be offered in their place some sparing generalisations on the unconscious motivations leading to the creation of the work in question. Nor is he likely to be mollified by the suggestion that anthropological studies of primitive art demonstrate convincingly the animistic and magical incentives to creative activity; or that all works of art must represent sublimations of primitive instincts; or that even the most utilitarian activities are influenced by sublimated energies and are to that extent works of art. There is however no way out of this dilemma. The dynamic psychologist studying the end-products of mental activity can see no valid reason to exclude art from the disciplines of scientific investigation, or to abandon the assumption that all mental activities are traceable in the last resort to common unconscious factors, and that consequently a man's dreams, hobbies, character, career, the implements he uses, his very signature can be legitimately regarded as works of art.

It is clear at any rate that any psychologist who claims to uncover the nature of mental activity must be prepared to brook a certain amount of æsthetic resentment from those whose attitude to creative activity is essentially religious. On the other hand a psychological system which cannot throw some light on the nature of art is scarcely deserving of the name. For this amongst other reasons it is appropriate to scan Jungian formulations on this subject.

Jung's earlier pronouncements on creative art were comparatively unambitious, consisting mainly of a few psycho-biological reflections of a very simple kind. On the assumption that some of the energy of producing eggs and sperma is transposed into the creation of mechanisms for allurement and for the protection of the young, Jung maintained that we 'discover the first instance of art in animals used in the service of the impulse of creation and limited to the breeding season'. He was careful however to qualify the extension of this view to man. 'Even if there can be no doubt about the sexual origin of music, still it would be a poor unæsthetic generalization if one were to include music in the category of sensuality.' Nevertheless: 'There are few things in life which cannot be reduced in the last analysis to the instinct of procreation.' For the rest his earlier concern with the creative artist was confined to some generalizations on the subject of phantasy. Phantasy, he maintained, is causally explained as a symptom of a physiological or personal condition. A symbol purposively seeks a clear and definite goal with the help of existing material; it strives to lay hold of a certain line for the future psychic development. Active phantasy is a principal attribute of the artistic mentality. The artist is thus not only a representer but a creator 'hence essentially an educator'. To this Jung added that the more abnormal the individual, the more limited will be the common social value of the symbols he produces. But apart from maintaining somewhat arbitrary distinctions between 'phantasm' and imaginative activity, including under this latter heading both active and passive varieties of 'phantasy', there is little to indicate the ultimate form of his analysis of creative art.

When in later years Jung expanded his views on this subject, his psychological system, including the concept of the Collective Unconscious, of the 'laws' of opposites and compensations and of the prospective nature of archetypical products, had already taken its final shape and had been correlated with alchemical philosophy, with the 'religious outlook' and with the Jungian process of 'individuation'. It is not surprising therefore to find that his views on artistic creation do little more than paraphrase his general outline of psychic function. In fact his views on art can scarcely be distinguished from his views on religion, sociology and politics.

But whereas in the case of sociology Jung maintains that the psychologist may legitimately seek to explore and explain the psychic factors responsible for group manifestations, in the case of art, he adopts in the first instance a *non-possumus* attitude that appears peculiarly timid if not peculiarly modest. Despite a bold preamble in which he states that the human psyche is 'the womb of all the sciences and arts', Jung appears to wash his hands of the responsibility of explaining these psychic manifestations. If, he says, the psychologist could be relied on to uncover the causal connections within a work of art and in the process of artistic creation, he would leave the study of art no ground to stand on and would reduce it to a special branch of his own science. Not content with this frivolous excuse for ignorance, Jung proceeds to close the door more firmly. 'The creative aspect of life which finds its clearest (sic) expression in art baffles all attempts at rational formulation.' And again: 'creative art will for ever elude understanding'. Here he introduces that frequently quoted aphorism which seems to be accounted to him for grace rather than for obscurantism—'a psychic product is something in or for itself, whether the work of art or the artist himself is in question'. 'Creativeness' he goes on, 'like the freedom of the will contains a secret . . . creative man is a riddle that we try to solve in vain.'

Further investigation shews however that Jung's assertion of the psychologist's incapacity to solve the secret of artistic creation is due neither to timidity nor to modesty. The secret is that there is no secret; or rather it is a secret only in so far as creation is an autonomous process contributed by the Collective Unconscious and independent of personal factors. Here Jung pauses to bestow a buffet on what he conceives to be Freudian theories of art. Taking literary productions as paradigmatic, he divides them into two groups, the psychological and the visionary. The former deal with con-

scious, comprehensible and familiar factors existing in the
'foreground' of life. Visionary factors on the other hand deal
with the 'hinterland' suggesting not only an abyss of time
separating us from prehuman ages but even abysses 'separating man from what has not yet become'; they arise from
primordial experience surpassing the understanding of man
who is indeed in danger of succumbing to them. They are
enormous, timeless and foreign, cold, many-sided, daemonic
and grotesque. If, Jung argues, we insist on deriving visionary products from personal experience we not only reduce
visionary art to a pathological and neurotic level at which
it functions as a substitute for some basic personal love
experience which is contrary to the spirit of the ego, but
also strip creative art of its primordial quality. It becomes
'nothing but a symptom' 'pregnant chaos shrinks to the
proportions of a psychic disturbance'. 'Abysses are dismissed
as illusions.' 'The work of art is conjured away', and we are
left with 'the psychic disposition of the poet himself'.

In passing it is curious to note how this travesty of Freud's
views on art has gained currency amongst those writers on
the psychology of art who are unversed in Freudian theory.
The elaborate history of unconscious sublimation, whereby
the frustrated energies of infantile libido are profoundly
modified and deflected towards a diversity of individual and
social ends, the individual origin and function of unconscious
phantasy and the intricate evolution therefrom of pre-conscious ideation and expression, the protean manifestations
of unconscious conflict and the complicated series of psychic
manoeuvres whereby conflict can be assuaged and the harshness of existence rendered more endurable, in a word all
those psycho-analytical formulations without which it is impossible even to grapple with the problem of artistic expression are summarily misrepresented by Jung in the statement that psycho-analysis regards art as pathological or neurotic. Visionary experience, says Jung, vigorously attacking
this Aunt Sally he has himself created, is not a symptom,
it is a deeper and more expressive experience than human

passion ' . . . an expression of something existent in its own right'.

But it is unnecessary to dwell again on Jung's favourite misconceptions of Freudian psychology or on the fact that Jung cannot understand the difference between conscious and unconscious mental activity. It is sufficient to quote in this connection his astonishing statements that 'human passion falls within the sphere of conscious experience' and that the subject of vision 'lies beyond' the sphere of conscious experience. If this astonishing collocation of ideas means anything it implies either that human passion has no unconscious roots, a preposterous claim, or that the Collective Unconscious, which by Jungian definition represents the tendencies inherited from our ancestors, has somehow or other come down to us shorn of the experience of human passion; that in fact our primitive ancestors were either Gods (and demons) or asexual. Yet if Jung's remark that art is a thing in itself is not to be dismissed as a commonplace meaning merely that it is an *end-product* like handwriting or a kitchen cupboard, it surely implies that the artistic impulse is an autonomous and impersonal psychic force having a psychic reality all its own, in other words, that it behaves in a way precisely similar to that of the Jungian Collective Unconscious.

And this is apparently what Jung does think. Forgetting those earlier times when in his view music had a sexual origin and when most things could be traced to the procreative instincts of man, he now tells us that individual passion is irrelevant to visionary art, which consists of intuitions of a dark nocturnal world peopled by demons, spirits and Gods, of a hidden, unknown and unknowable and to the ordinary mortal terrifying chaos of primordial tendencies which can obtain only mythological expression. It has itself no words, no images and can only be seen in a glass darkly. Then comes the categorical statement 'that which appears in vision is Collective Unconscious . . . psychic disposition shaped by the forces of heredity'. The 'life-giving

171

secret of man' is that this vision-producing system has 'a purposiveness outreaching human ends'. It is compensatory to the conscious system and 'can bring a one-sided, abnormal or dangerous state of consciousness into equilibrium in an apparently purposive way'.

At this point Jung links up his aesthetic with his sociological formulations. The artist's intuitions and visions arising from the purposive Collective Unconscious are shared by seers, prophets, leaders and enlighteners. An epoch is like an individual. Each period has its bias, its prejudice and its psychic ailment calling for compensatory adjustment. This is effected by the Collective Unconscious in that 'a poet, a seer or a leader allows himself to be guided by the unexpressed desire of his times and shows the way by word or deed to the attainment of that which everyone blindly craves and expects whether this results in good or evil, the healing of an epoch or its destruction'. When, as in the case of Goethe, the Collective Unconscious becomes a living experience and is brought to bear on the conscious outlook of an age 'this event is a creative act of importance to everyone living in that age'.

Translating all this in terms of works of art Jung reaches the conclusion that 'what is essential in a work of art is that it should rise far above the realm of personal life and speak from the spirit and *heart* of the poet *as man* to the spirit and *heart of mankind*' (author's italics). So after all the passion of man is both personal and impersonal. Nevertheless, the personal aspect of artistic creation, 'is a limitation and even a sin in the realm of art'. In the same breath, we are told that every creative person is a duality, a synthesis of contradictory attitudes arising from personal life and from an impersonal creative process. Nevertheless, 'Art is an innate drive that seizes a human being and makes him its instrument'. The artist, Jung adds, is Collective Man carrying and shaping the unconscious psychological life of mankind. The conflicts and insufficiencies of the artist's personal life are 'regrettable results of the fact that he is an artist'. The
172

creative process is in any case a feminine quality arising from the unconscious depths, 'from the realm of mothers'. Yet, hermaphroditically enough, primordial images, e.g., of the Wise Man, Saviour or Redeemer 'dormant since the dawn of culture' do not appear in the dreams of individuals or in the works of art until called out by the waywardness of the general outlook; and this despite the fact that the waywardness of the individual artist is not, according to Jung, a factor in his art but a consequence of it. No matter: the secret of artistic creation and of the effectiveness of art is to be found in a return to the state of *participation mystique*.

It will be seen that once cleared of the transcendental spinach with which they are coated, Jung's theories contribute nothing to the understanding of art. His pronouncements regarding artistic creation are in fact of interest mainly as sidelights on his psychological theories. In particular they confirm the view put forward earlier in this essay, that Jung's spiritual home is in the conscious psychology of the pre-Freudian epoch, and that he seeks to get rid of those embarrassing manifestations of unconscious function which call for explanation in terms of individual development by projecting them into an alleged Collective 'Unconscious' where they acquire autonomy, overwhelming force, unknowableness, blindness, darkness, perspicacity, prospectiveness, wisdom, insight, foresight, pedagogic power, compensatoriness, equilibristic faculties and tertiary sexual characterisitcs. Being incapable of recognizing or understanding the unconscious ego and its relation to man's primitive instinctual inheritance (in Freudian terms, the *Id*), Jung fathers a new animism by fusing the manifestations of both Ego and Id and projecting the amalgam into a psychic concept 'the collective archetype' which is indistinguishable from the 'idea of God'. The dangerous unknowableness experienced, according to Jung, in artistic

173

visions cannot in fact be distinguished from the *numinosum* which gives rise to the Jungian 'religious outlook'. *This at least is one of the secrets of the Jungian system, that its founder has mistaken the unconscious ego for God and on the strength of this 'discovery' has founded Neo-animism.*

It is a natural consequence of Jung's projection of primitive characteristics forth of the ego that he discounts heavily the personal factor in creative art. It has already been observed that Jung's attitude to the mental disabilities or weaknesses of man is little short of contemptuous. He is constantly complaining of the babyishness of the ordinary man, although to be sure he maintains that babies and younglings have no problems to speak of, a state of affairs which, if true, would suggest that adult man undergoes a rapid deterioration on coming of age. Moreover it is significant that the 'individuation' Jung values so highly should be regarded by him as a characteristic of 'rarer spirits' and, in any case, a manifestation of the second half of life. Whether this devaluation of individual factors is due to fear or to nihilism or to both, Jung certainly carries it to its logical conclusion by denying individual man whatever credit or comfort he might derive from his artistic achievements. Granted that to Jung a personal factor is little more than a conscious element, at most a superficial manifestation of the (Freudian) pre-conscious, he has nevertheless postulated a 'personal unconscious' which, it would seem, plays no part in creative art. Here again we see the cloven hoof of the conscious psychologist, namely an obsession with the adult. Like 'economic man', the 'artist' is regarded as a purely adult manifestation, springing into being with only 'collective' antecedents. Whereas if anything is obvious about the psychology of art it is that without an elaborate and exhaustive investigation of the artistic achievements of children from the cradle to puberty it must be an arid and mainly descriptive pursuit leading only to sterile conclusions regarding adult function. At no time does Jung shew the slightest regard for developmental factors. A child's mind is

174

a closed book to him; although if there is an atom of value in the concept of the Collective Unconscious it would surely suggest that the individual youth of man is as fateful for his ultimate development as his racial youth. It is in fact a field of research in its own right deserving of urgent priority.

Even more intriguing are the difficulties that arise when one attempts to square Jung's theories of art with his theories of attitudinal and functional types, of superior and inferior functions, and of the reciprocal and compensatory relations existing between the Collective unconscious and ego-consciousness. Jung denies, for example, the intrinsic importance of the psychological novel, as compared with the products of visionary writers, amongst whom incidentally he persists in including Rider Haggard. The former is concerned with psychological interpretations of the 'foreground of life' the latter with visionary interpretations of the 'hinterland'. But according to his theories of character types the extraverted novelist, who is none the less extraverted because he writes of the inner motivations of others, may well be a frustrated introvert who has neglected his intuitive function. And by the Jungian law of compensation, he may be struggling to correct the dangers of a too one-sided Collective Unconscious by the expedient of substituting analysis for vision. Laudably enough, for if we are to believe Jung a supercharged Collective Unconscious may be responsible for either neurosis or insanity. Nowhere indeed is it more apparent that Jung's psychological progress has been constantly hampered by lack of clear thinking and an incapacity to correlate his scattered generalisations concerning mental function. Although he displayed considerable alacrity in throwing over his Freudian convictions, he has rarely shewn any capacity to discard those parts of his own theory which are incompatible with what appear to be his main theses regarding psychic activity. On the contrary, he has clung to his favourite psychological preoccupations with character and compensation regardless of their mutual contradictoriness and of their incompatibility with the concept of a prospective Collective Unconscious. The results are as baffling as they are vexatious to the inquiring reader.

But although Jung's formulations on art are interesting mainly as additional illustrations of his lifeless, one-dimensional approach to the problems of human personality, which by his reckoning is in itself void of creative power, there is one respect in which they are deserving of attention from the student of aesthetics. As has been suggested the recent tendency to employ in the study of art techniques of interpretation based on the discovery of the unconscious mind has induced many writers on aesthetics to eke out by their own efforts the paucity of contributions on this subject by specialists versed in unconscious psychology. Speaking of the scientific approach to creative art and in particular of the influence of rationalism on programmatic Surrealism, J. P. Hodin remarks[1] that this is a case of 'the shadow of psychoanalysis falling on art'. Unfortunately most writers have no very clear idea of the gulf between the concept of the unconscious as employed by Freud and Jung respectively, with the result that a good deal of unnecessary misunderstanding and misconception arises. It is the more necessary therefore to reiterate that there is no possible connection between the unconscious of Freud and that of Jung, and that, particularly in the case of Surrealism, it is not the shadow of psychoanalysis that has fallen on art but the shadow of the Jungian Collective Unconscious.

An excellent example of the confusion is provided by Glicksberg[2] in his essay on Surrealism; 'Then comes the liberating discovery of the unconscious . . . If we believe in the revelations of the unconscious, then dreams have predictive value; they are symbols of a higher creative truth: cries from the depth, primordial images, oracular manifestations of the subliminal life. Henceforth if we have but the courage to possess ourselves of the Surrealist faith, we can live in a golden, fantastic dream-world. Irresponsibility is

[1] *Horizon*, January 1949.
[2] Op. Cit.

King, the unconscious is law'. But all this has nothing to do with the unconscious discovered by Freud. It is almost but not entirely pure Jung; not entirely, because the 'subliminal' of Jung pertains to his personal not his Collective Unconscious. And again Glicksberg referring to the 'evil forces of the unconscious' says 'We repress these powerful instincts because we are ashamed of them, because we fear them'. But this is sheer Jung and has not the remotest connection with repression, which is a purely unconscious mechanism activated by unconscious fears and guilts. And yet again 'The contents of the unconscious, however . . . are composed of private subjective elements, the jetsam and flotsam of personal impressions and experiences'. This is neither good Freud nor good Jung. Jung's system centres round the Collective Unconscious which is quite impersonal, and it is Jung who is responsible for the view that Freud's unconscious is flotsam and jetsam.

Still further confusion is introduced by those accredited protagonists of Surrealism who believe, as does Herbert Read, that 'it is only now, with the aid of modern psychology, in the name of Marx and Freud that they (poets and painters) have found themselves in a position to put their beliefs and practices on a scientific basis'. Despite an enthusiastic regard for Freud and plentiful quotation from his works, Herbert Read not only fails to grasp the unconscious nature of repression but takes a near-Jungian view of unconscious function. Surrealism, for him, is a 'reaffirmation of the romantic principle'; and the romantic spirit in turn is the principle of life, creation and liberation, in contrast to the classical spirit which is a principle of 'order, of control and of repression'. 'If we are conscious of our instincts and repress them then we act under duress and produce nothing but intellectual reactions'.

That this is a characteristically Jungian position is borne out by Read's further statements that 'sublimation involves a conformity to collective ideals', whereas in fact sublimation is an unconscious process unconsciously achieved at a time

177

when the child dwells under familial influences; it involves a process of desexualisation of infantile instinct which is only in part the direct result of environmental stress. That Read is thinking of adult Collective influences is clear from his insistence that instincts are repressed in the interest of values which represent 'defences of some particular structure of society, the rule of some particular class.'

It is not surprising therefore to find Read subscribing to broader Jungian generalizations without apparently being aware that he is thereby abandoning his Freudian allegiances. Thus the artist according to him offers society some knowledge of the secrets to which he has had access and which 'he alone can reveal in all their actuality'. 'The more we learn about the unconscious the more collective it appears to be.' It is, here he quotes Grierson, 'a body of common sentiments and universal truths'. The truths of romanticism, he continues, are coeval with the growing consciousness of mankind. Again although unlike Jung, he distinguishes between the manifest and the latent content of dreams, Read follows the Jungian tradition when he speaks of 'weaving its (the dream's) reality into the synthesis of our art'. The dream 'transforms' the day world. Hence the conclusion that 'between the surreal and the supernatural, there is only a difference of age, of evolution'. In short the more one studies the efforts of enthusiastic amateurs to apply 'psychological principles' to the problem of art, the more obvious it becomes that they operate on the strength of some vaguely apprehended and generally misunderstood concepts. There may indeed be a great future for a dynamic psychology of art, but this is certainly not the way to set about establishing it. In the meantime the only connection that can be traced between Freudian psychology and surrealism is a technical one, namely, the application by the artist either deliberately or spontaneously of a method of 'free presentation' which, however, has as much resemblance to 'free association' as has the technique of the confessional to the technique of psycho-analysis.

178

Nor does it help matters when, as will sometimes happen, clinical psychologists take the bit between their teeth and produce rule of thumb interpretations of works of art based on whatever views they may hold regarding unconscious content. A recent writer[1] examining seventy works of art, from primitive sculptures, such as the Venus of Willendorf, to the cartoons of David Low and the representations of Amino, Bauer, Calder, Dali, Ernst and Munch, and ignoring all conventional art-chronologies or stylistic classifications, has provided each of them with an interpretation of its unconscious content. If these various interpretations were strung together, they would provide an epitome of unconscious libido- and ego-development, based for the most part on Freudian theories plentifully tinctured however with Jungian ideology. And in fact Goitein maintains that only the intrinsic psycho-dynamic factors should determine the essential homogeneity of art classification.

All this gets us nowhere. Goitein admits that the illustrations are used simply as stimuli to the reader's own interpretations; anyone is free to transpose the source material as he chooses. So long as he interprets the manifest content of the creative work in terms of its latent content, i.e., in terms of different levels of mental unfolding, it doesn't seem to matter what particular illustration or stylistic expression he selects to prove his point. The only chronology that matters according to Goitein is that of the psyche. From the point of view of creative art, this is almost as nihilistic a view as Jung's attribution of visionary art to inherited psychic tendencies (the collective archetypes). Followed to its logical conclusion it raises the Rorschachian Inkblot[2] to the height of Absolute Art, or, according to the taste of the observer, reduces the archetypical idea of God

[1] Lionel Goitein. *Art and the Unconscious*. New York 1948.

[2] In the Rorschach Test which has achieved an increasing popularity amongst psychiatrists, the patient is shown standardized inkblot pictures; personality estimations are then arrived at by studying the images produced in response to these non-personal stimuli.

to the cultural level of an ink-blot stimulus. The emotional reaction to the work of art is regarded as a co-efficient of the unconscious urges of the artist and those of the observer.

But the curious part of Goitein's exposition is not so much the fact that he empties a cornucopia of unconscious interpretations over the heads of the art-aching[1] public or that he fuses the incompatible ideas of Freud and Jung, but that his interpretative glosses are woven together to form tapestries of unconscious content. Exhibitionism, oral-sadism, anal erotism, phallic omnipotence, the Id, the Super-ego, the Libido, the Oedipus situation, the castration complex, introjection, extraversion, sublimation, even the anima and the archetype are used as pigments to produce a surrealist picture of the unconscious psyche. In a word his interpretations turn to pictorial projections in his hands. The analyst becomes artist. This is a truly Jungian exploit, appearing to contradict the popular view that the analytical and the creative functions of the mind are incompatible.

Perhaps the truth of the matter is that some analysts have mistaken their vocation. No doubt too there are many bad artists who ought to have been bad novelists; certainly there are many bad novelists who might well have covered their creative deficiencies by becoming indifferent psychologists. Be all this as it may, the real test of an analytical psychologist is whether he can refrain from anthropomorphising his functional concepts. For should he give way to this temptation, the way is open to project into the concept such personal attributes as he finds himself unable to explain. Even the strictly disciplined Freudian finds himself beset with this temptation, referring on occasion to the Id as if it were an archaic ego-institution. Some indeed have gone so far as to postulate in the suckling such mental structure and content as would be appropriate in the two or three year old child. This is not psycho-analysis: it is a projective technique whereby the misguided analyst endows the infant

[1] When first the neolithic troglodyte
Art-aching loosed his after-dinner vest (George Fletcher).

with his own subjective phantasies both conscious and unconscious.

But at least it can be said in the psycho-analyst's favour that as a rule he is aware of this temptation and strives to withstand it. Jung, despite his early acquaintance with the theory and method of psycho-analysis, succumbed to the temptation. His first step on abandoning his devotion to Freudian theories was to reject these painfully acquired discoveries regarding the early instincts of the child and the elaborate stages of infantile development during which a variety of archaic endo-psychic mechanisms is employed to control them. Having taken this first step, the rest of his rake's progress was comparatively easy. All he had to do was to excogitate a non-personal concept into which he projected all those unconscious psychic characteristics of small children he was *ipso facto* unable to understand. Hence the Collective Unconscious.

It is not difficult to indicate yet another tendency which Jung shares with the artist. It is to project into the future a state of individual perfection the existence of which plainly cannot be substantiated in the present. This is the secret of his concept of 'individuation'. By Jung's own shewing, this 'state' is rarely attained and only then in the latter half of life; it is accompanied by, indeed produces, an etiolated capacity for love and the 'wisdom' it brings is a preparation for death. In short Jungian individuation presents all the clinical features of an illusion, a phantom carrot to be dangled before the nose of the inadequate and the dejected.

If we would understand the motives for these projections, we must consider the twofold nature of the asperities of life. To the intractability of our environmental conditions must be added the burden of that mental conflict, which is a co-efficient of the friction inevitably arising between instinctual forces and unconscious controlling agencies. To this perpetual clash between the pleasure-principle and the reality-principle, the unconscious ego reacts in two ways; first, by

181

seeking to project its painful excitations into the external world where it seems to find a 'real' cause for its 'pain', and, second, by seeking to modify the environment in a way that will render it more amenable to the demands of instinct. Since, however, under normal circumstances, other unconscious mental mechanisms prevent the *direct* expression of primitive instinct, the ultimate effect of this projection must always be in the nature of a compromise. Naturally the end-results of these projection devices varies. In one case they may give rise to a primitive animistic system in which 'spirits' or 'forces' residing in the inanimate can be placated or modified by magical procedures; in another they may give rise to a religious form in which a supernatural God can be appeased by sacrifice, acts of expiation, prayer, or good works. In yet another case it can obtain expression through the work of Art, a modification of environment in which mostly though not exclusively inanimate means are employed to represent the illusory and for the greater part symbolic gratification of the unconscious stresses to which the artist has been and is subject.

But whereas under ordinary circumstances the direction of projection is limited in the sense that it is canalised towards natural environment both animate and inanimate or towards ideas concerning external objects of instincts, it is open to the psychologist to develop new channels of projection. The conditions of projection are fulfilled as long as sources of internal psychic tension operating *within* the ego are 'objectivated', i.e., are held to exist *outside* the confines of the (unconscious or conscious) ego. As we have seen, by postulating the existence of *autonomous* collective forces operating on the ego from 'within' the total psyche, Jung satisfied the requirements of projection. For clearly the stimulations of the Jungian Collective Unconscious although 'within' the psyche are from the ego point of view 'without' the ego. Now it has been shewn that the archetypical content of the Collective Unconscious, which Jung alleges to be racial in origin, is in fact derived from the projection into

182

it of phantasy formations characteristic of early infantile stages of personal development. It is not hard to indicate the emotional drive leading to this projection. *It is an attempt to eject from the region of the unconscious ego the painful stimulations of unconscious conflict.*

To those who are ready and anxious to be comforted by illusions, this is no doubt a highly laudable procedure. And no doubt it accounts in part for the popularity of Jungian doctrine. But from the point of view of the advancement of science it is a reactionary and obscurantist device. The discovery of unconscious conflict was Freud's major contribution to mental science; and to the extent that psycho-analysis offers some prospect of its solution however partial, it may be said to have offered humanity legitimate hopes in place of deceptions and disguises. Any attempt to reverse the course of psycho-analytical discovery and, by obscuring the individual nature of unconscious conflict, to set back the clock of psychological progress is a signal disservice to those who desire, however timidly, to cultivate a sense of Reality.

Having embarked on a comparative assessment of Freudian and Jungian views on art, it is desirable to conclude with some considerations of a more general nature, bearing on the relations of psycho-analysis to art. For it is obvious that even if Jung's theory were accurate, namely, that visionary art is a contribution from the Collective Unconscious projected on to the environment through the agency of the individual 'seer', it would still merely touch the fringe of the problem. Although projection is one of the earliest modes of function of the mental apparatus and flourishes at a period when no clear distinction exists between ego and non-ego or between the self and the outer world of objects, it is after all only one of a number of unconscious dynamic mechanisms by means of which the unconscious ego seeks to regulate its instinctual stresses. Only in the hallucinatory products of the infantile dream can we observe the comparatively isolated functioning of the projection mechanism. By the time the infant has passed the stage of inarticulate cries and can give some organized expression to its emotional states in rudimentary words, the mental apparatus has reached a stage of development at which it is impossible for *unmodified* instinctual tensions to be projected. The processes of *compromise-formation* whereby repressed and repressing forces can obtain expression in one and the same product has already become a fine psychic art, which receives its most striking illustration in the symptom-formations of the infantile neurosis. Even the projections of the adult schizophrenic are represented in a highly disguised form and bear witness to the operation of those secondary processes which are characteristic of the more superficial pre-conscious layers of the mind.

It follows therefore that although the magical aim of the work of art obtains its maximum expression through projective techniques, as can be easily observed in the songs, dances, paintings and sculptures of primitive man and in child's art-play, the more sophisticated work of art has many other tasks to perform. It must not only represent the kernel phantasies giving rise to conflict in the mind of the artist, but also the expiation or negation of these same phantasies. In so doing it makes use of those infinitively complex defensive processes which affect the instinctual force at every stage of its passage from the Id, through the unconscious and preconscious ego, to the field of perceptual consciousness. In the last stages of the journey, the processes of 'secondary elaboration' and 'rationalization' take effect, cementing the compromise in such a way that the onlooker is more or less prepared to assimilate the artist's work. In this connection it is of interest that the average surrealist picture, although apparently devoid of secondary elaboration, is in fact more rationalized than the most classical products of classical painting. In two respects therefore the work of art represents a compromise, first, between the repressed and the repressing forces, and, second, between

184

the primary and the secondary processes of mind.[1]

And here perhaps is the point at which a fundamental confusion as to the relation of art to the neuroses or to the subjective peculiarities of the artist can be cleared up. To say that a work of art is a *ding an sich*, a thing in its own right, means no more than that it is a specific and characteristic mode of instinctual expression, a characteristic end-product. By the same token a neurosis exists in its own right, a fact which, however does not entitle us to regard a work of art as an essentially pathological product. No doubt there are many resemblances between the two end-products. Certainly the neurotic exhibits considerable unconscious skill in building up his neurotic compromise. Some obsessional neuroses, for example, illustrate the operation of advanced artistic techniques. And there are no doubt many art products which bear the hallmark of neurotic and other varieties of pathological mechanism. There is however one essential difference between the pure work of art and the neurosis. The neurosis is the result of a *regression* of libido leading to the *breakdown* of a repression system which is *already* faulty, hence the emergence of compromises between the repressed and the repressing forces. It is also an unconscious instrument of self-punishment. Whatever its original unconscious aim, the work of art represents a *forward* urge of the libido seeking to maintain its hold on the world of objects. Its instinctual compromises are not the result of a pathological breakdown of the repression system. Rather it acts as an auxiliary device to maintain the efficiency of repression. It is in the truest sense a sublimation. and consequently obviates the need for self-punishment.

As for the alleged personal idiosyncracies of the artist it can only be said that so far little scientific work has been done on the subject; and that in any case no effective controls have been established, e.g., by taking random and selected samples of the incidence of neurotic or other peculiarities amongst non-artists, and of creative expression

[1] See p. 13.

amongst 'normal' persons. We may reasonably suspect that
a good deal of subjective prejudice has crept into the discussion of the subject; and not a little myth formation of the
kind which attributes secret drinking to our Prime Min-
isters. In any case there is no particular reason to single out
the artist as a victim of the debunker's passionate art. The
correlation of psycho-pathological manifestations with the
attributes of genius is no doubt, to use Jung's expression,
an interesting subject for investigation. But until it has been
so investigated we do well to suspend judgement. In the
meantime we have one sure criterion by means of which
we can distinguish art from psycho-pathology. Unconscious
conflict is an inevitable consequence of the instinctual inheritance of man who seeks to stem its more impossible
demands with every means at his disposal. Reinforcing the
defensive mechanism of sublimation, the artist seeks to
maintain his own peace of mind through his creative work,
and at the same time is capable of bringing some 'peace
through catharsis' to the minds of others. The neurotic,
owing to constitutional peculiarities and developmental
vicissitudes is unable to sustain himself on his sublimations
and unconsciously casts the die in favour of regression. In
the end he punishes himself and not infrequently his
family and familiars. The neurotic artist seeks a double
compromise. Struggling to effect through artistic sublimations a balanced solution of his unconscious conflict, he
nevertheless cripples these efforts by having recourse at the
same time to neurotic symptom-formations which may
ultimately interfere with his artistic technique, his choice
of subject or both. Only in exceptional cases can this double
compromise be effective. As a rule the unfortunate victim
falls between two stools, being neither a good artist nor a
successful neurotic.

CHAPTER XI

CONCLUSION: THE ECLECTIC'S DILEMMA

'At the bottom of the advocacy of a dual doctrine slumbers the idea that there is no harm in men being mistaken, or at least only so little harm as is more than compensated for by the marked tranquility in which their mistake may wrap them.'

'Men leave error undisturbed, because they accept in a loose way the proposition that a belief may be "morally useful without being intellectually sustainable".'

John Morley: 'On Compromise'.

THE psychological eclectic is accustomed to defend his hotch-potch of theories on the ground that, standing aloof from the heat and dust of controversy, he is the better able to assess the virtues and weaknesses of the various 'schools' of clinical psychology. Having singled out the 'good' points of all sides, he proceeds to build up a patchwork system which, he feels, must somehow or another lie near to the truth of the matter. And no doubt he is sincerely convinced that in psychological affairs the truth can be arrived at by calculating the Highest Common Factor of contrasting systems. A plethora of expository surveys of 'modern' psychology bears witness to the fact that eclecticism is generally regarded as a form of objectivity, reflecting credit on those who cultivate it. This is a view which the casual reader, always inclined to see fair play and confusing eclecticism with impartiality, feels strongly disposed to support. Believing that there must be at least two sides to any question, he finds it hard to conceive that one side may rest on total error. And so, in the case of the Freud-Jung controversy he is ready to dismiss any sustained *ex-parte* criticism as a sign of obstinacy and fanaticism if not of positive weakness.

There are of course all sorts of eclectic. The term denotes not any coherent school of thought, but merely a class of unclassifiables having in common a perhaps excessive dis-

187

regard for the claims of logical consistency. Among them are many useful persons, aiming at, and in favourable cases obtaining, quick therapeutic results; or, at worst, intervening between the sufferer on the one hand and on the other the massed misunderstandings and moral indignation of his family, his family doctor and himself.

Besides this practical and pedestrian kind of eclectic we have a sublimer race of beings whose only discernible object is to astound. These very often affect a sort of super-Freudianism mixed up with anything else they fancy. A favourite dodge is to pity and revile Freud for his initial 'errors' with the implication that these errors were ultimately corrected not by Freud but by the triumphant super-Freudian and his allies. Ready with the pen, they are accustomed to produce weighty textbooks that are widely read by those who find comfort in pointing to the existence of warring 'schools' and concluding therefrom that because Jung and Adler disagreed with Freud the monumental structure of Freud's unconscious psychology must rest on shaky foundations.

For all practical purposes, however, we may divide the eclectics into two groups, the academic and the psychiatric. The academic psychologist having little or no experience of mental disorder apparently feels that he is thereby qualified to render dispassionate judgement on the respective validity of Freudian or Jungian concepts. But since his lack of first hand experience or training prevents his acquiring any understanding of unconscious mental function, his opinions carry little weight outside the academic field; and since his students are also concerned exclusively with the conscious manifestations of mental activity, the academic eclectic is harmless enough.

Psychiatric eclectics are birds of a different feather. Having an extensive though blindfold acquaintance with the insanities and occupying vantage points in the administration of mental health services and of training centres, they can seriously hamper the development of psychological science. At the risk therefore of appearing unduly partisan, and thereby arousing the reader's sympathy for an oppressed cause, it is necessary to restate in conclusion the reasons why the Freud-Jung issue cannot be blanketed by eclectic compromises.

In the first place it should be made clear that when basic principles are at stake, there can be no question of arriving at a gentleman's agreement. It is not hard to imagine what astronomical confusion would have arisen had the eclectics of the period insisted on supporting compromises between the Ptolemaic and the Copernican systems. As Jung himself remarked 'He whose sun still revolves around the earth is a different person from him whose earth is the satellite of the Sun'. The issue between Freud and Jung is of a similar degree of magnitude and is as refractory to compromise. If Freud is right, Jung is nothing more or less than an academic (conscious) psychologist masquerading as the apostle of a new dynamic psychology. If Jung is right, Freud's system should be dismissed as the symptomatic expression of a psycho-pathological character, valid only for those who suffer from similar obsessions.

Throughout this essay attention has been concentrated on those basic concepts of the Freudian and Jungian systems which illustrate their mutual incompatibility; and an endeavour has been made to set forth as simply as possible the technical reasons why they are so incompatible. In summing up these arguments, it is desirable however to restate the position in more general terms. Thus one of the main issues at stake is whether psychology should revert to its original status as handmaiden to logic and metaphysics or whether it should cling to its dearly won title to be regarded as a science in its own right. So long as mind and consciousness were regarded as co-terminous, it was impossible to contest the authority of the metaphysician, who was therefore in a position to hamper the development of psychological science by introducing whatever supernatural or transcendental considerations might appeal to him. And to this day the greatest obstacle to psychological understanding

189

is the persistent belief that the conscious or at most the pre-conscious mind comprises for all practical purposes the totality of mental activity.

Freud's discovery of the dynamic unconscious, his for-mulation of the laws that govern this part of the psychic apparatus, his description of the origin and development of the unconscious ego and of the various components of primitive instinct which it seeks to regulate, were the first and decisive steps towards the building up of a scientific psychology. For the first time it was possible to understand the part played by psychic conflict in accelerating the development of specifically human characteristics; for the first time the staggering achievements of child-develop-ment could be assessed at their proper value, and the majority of adult mental disorders recognized as measures of the failure of the child to overcome the odds with which it is faced; for the first time it was possible to hold out some hope that by adjustment of earlier difficulties, the adult mind might be freed to carry out its tasks of adaptation.

As we have seen the most consistent trend of Jungian psychology is its negation of every important part of Freudian theory. The Freudian unconscious is abolished and in its place we are presented with that shallow pre-conscious system described by Jung as the Personal Unconscious. Having eliminated the dynamic unconscious and being unable to discover in his Personal Unconscious forces and mechanisms that would account for man's psychic activities, Jung looks for the mainspring of mind in a purely con-stitutional factor—the Collective Unconscious. By so doing he closes the door against any possibility of discovering the unconscious ego, and at the same time abolishes the concept of individual unconscious conflict. Conflict is reduced to an opposition between constitutional tendencies and the volitional aspects of consciousness. To make assurance doubly sure a system of opposites and compensations is postulated which abolishes any dynamic distinction between the Collective Unconscious and consciousness.

190

This nihilistic approach to the facts of mental development is further reinforced by the Jungian concept of mental energy which does away with the necessity of investigating infantile life and at the same time reduces conflict to the level of a conscious problem. With the introduction of his monistic *élan vital*, moving like a neutral force from one position to another, from the Collective Unconscious to the Persona and back, the whole concept of instinctual modification and with it the concept of infantile conflict goes by the board. Inevitably unconscious psychic mechanisms lose any distinctive characteristics they possess and are reduced to mere centripetal and centrifugal movements of mental energy in a closed system. In any case there is no room in the Jungian psychology for concepts such as repression which are totally incompatible with the automatic operation of laws of opposites and compensations.

The petrifying influence of these Jungian postulates is nowhere more obvious than in his theories of mental disorder. Having eliminated the unconscious ego and the specific defence mechanisms at its control and having flattened out the distinction between primary and secondary psychic processes, Jung leaves us to assume that neuroses are the result of psychic automatisms. That he attributes the neuroses to a failure to perform a 'life-task' is at best a placebo to beguile the patient's conscious ego, at worst a smoke-screen to cover the automatic activities of a Collective Unconscious which operates either as a dæmonic and disruptive force or, in the more favourable instance, as a vocational instrument of predestination. Even the alleged 'prospective' tendencies of the Jungian Unconscious represent a constitutionally pre-determined 'wisdom', which we are supposed to neglect at our peril.

Similarly in the case of Jungian character formation; this is regulated by automatic and reversible movements of the *élan vital* acting in combination with a fixed set of faculties to produce a fixed set of permutations and combinations. Such changes of character as may arise during the

191

course of life are in turn determined by the 'stage' of life at which the individual (if indeed he be an individual and not a loosely strung combination of the Jungian persona with ego-consciousness), has arrived. The infinite variability of human character, the endless shifts, ventures, and expedients to which, under the spur of unconscious conflict, the mind has recourse and which can give drama and dignity to its operations, are reduced to the level of a puppet-show, in which the Collective Unconscious automatically pulls the strings. This is the essence of Jungian psychology.

And this is where the eclectic, however ingenious or facile his mental processes, can fairly be asked to stand and render verdict. If he is to retain any shred of scientific self-respect, he must abandon the attempt to have it both ways. He must in fact make up his mind. He must declare whether he accepts the fundamental Freudian concepts of the unconscious mind, or whether he prefers to cling to pre-Freudian views which were based on the conviction that mind and consciousness are synonymous. For there is no other alternative. Reject the Freudian unconscious and, however elaborately the rejection is buttressed by acceptance of Jungian, Adlerian, Stekelian, Rankian or Kleinian systems, the result is the same; the eclectic reveals himself a conscious psychologist. Appeals to some elaborate system of constitutional factors however speciously these may be expressed in psycho-biological, psychological, metaphysical or mystical terms will avail him nothing. The Freudian concept of the unconscious is the basis of dynamic psychology. So far without exception, attempts to 'water it down' or 'improve' it have ended in diluting it or improving it out of existence. One may take it or one may leave it; but one cannot possibly do both at the same time.

Nor should the eclectic flatter himself that by accepting bits and pieces of the Jungian system he is thereby adding to the 'spiritual' value of his hybrid psychology or avoiding that form of psychic determinism which he feels to be the main stumbling block in Freudian theory. For by so doing he is merely escaping from the frying-pan to the fire. Jung's psychological system is in fact the most rigidly deterministic system that can possibly be conceived. Unleavened by hope and excluding even the 'Grace of God', it outvies those early theological doctrines according to which original sin could be stemmed only through fear of Divine Wrath. In place of original sin we have the dæmonic force of the Collective Unconscious which can be overcome only by an alliance between the Collective Unconscious and ego-consciousness and if possible a belief in the numinous idea of God. The psychic determinism of Freud at least permits man to hope that in the unending struggles between Id impulse and Ego-adaptation, the victories gained during early development may stand him in good stead. Even if the amount of 'freed-will' accruing therefrom is only marginal, it at any rate allows man the freedom to decide to continue the struggle. The Jungian Odyssey of individuation leaves man in the end with the task of dying gracefully with or without a sustaining belief in the idea of immortality.

The discovery that Jung is a conscious psychologist provides a happy solution of the problem that faces every writer who ventures to take up an uncompromising attitude on matters of psychological controversy. Sustained destructive criticism inevitably provokes in the reader a generous impulse to defend the weaker side. In this case there is no weaker side. The issue between Freud and Jung on close inspection proves to be no issue. There is no means of compromising between a theory of mind based on unconscious psychology and one based on an exclusively conscious psychology. And so we are left with the pleasant task of appraising Jung's position as a conscious psychologist. For there is no doubt that, after a fruitful period when Jung produced his studies on dementia præcox and on word association tests, his reputation as a clinical psychiatrist dwindled to vanishing point. True, his later work on alchemy exhibited

193

some of his former flair; and had he not been concerned to find in Hermetic philosophy forerunners of his own 'analytical psychology', his publications on the former subject would have stood as works of reference.

To estimate accurately Jung's position as a conscious psychologist it is necessary to single out his qualifications for this variety of psychological activity, offsetting these with any obvious handicaps he may manifest. Now the most we can expect of a conscious psychologist is that he should be a sound observer with a flair for classification, an eye for statistical error and if possible a capacity to draw useful conclusions from his data of observation. He need not have any particular flair for interpretation. Indeed a capacity for interpretation is rather a drawback to the conscious psychologist; for sooner or later it will lead him to make inferences which can only be substantiated by the techniques of unconscious psychology—a distinctly embarrassing contingency.

Study of Jung's published works proves beyond doubt that he is possessed of some unusual qualifications and some unusual handicaps. In the first place he is undoubtedly an indefatigable worker and is prepared to pursue his investigations in fields frequently neglected by the conscious psychologist. Next to the study of children, of neurotics and of the insane, anthropology provides the most fruitful field of psychological observation. Jung, as we have seen, knows next to nothing about children, and has been led astray by his observations of the neuroses and psychoses; but in the formal though not in the dynamic or interpretative sense he is a good anthropologist. Indeed it is remarkable that having embarked on this work, he should have produced such banal conclusions. And one is compelled to believe that, to use his own terminology, the difficulty lay in an opposition between his ritualistic and his imaginative sides. Apparently however he is unable to achieve the solution of this difficulty he recommends to others, namely, the 'merging' of the opposites. For his psychological writings are
194

hidebound with ritualism and at the same time display an ungovernable tendency to phantasy thinking. Perhaps the 'mystical' nature of much of his theorising is a compensation for his rigidity of thought; perhaps the rigidity of his classifications is a disciplinary compensation for his undisciplined fancies. Who but a Jungian could decide on this matter? The conclusion in any case is the same. Jung has the makings of a good conscious psychologist but suffers from a lack of disciplined control that serves to stultify his more positive qualifications. How else can one explain his general woolliness, vagueness and frequent equivocations?

Clearly then Jung is himself somewhat of an enigma. And perhaps the most charitable explanation of his failure as a psychologist is that he is a self-frustrated romantic trying to be an artist. Whether or not he has succeeded must be left to those aesthetically qualified to judge. Apart from the opportunities afforded by the presentation of case-histories and the balanced exposition of theory, the field of scientific psychology does not lend itself to artistic expression. What it does afford the disgruntled is an unrivalled opportunity to play the pedagogue. And this opportunity Jung has seized with both hands. When his theories have been forgotten and his anthropological work duly indexed in bibliographies, quotations from his more scholastic utterances will no doubt still adorn the works of those eclectic psychologists who cannot refrain from instructing their charges and the world at large in the way they should go. For the ultimate dilemma of the eclectic is whether or not he should accept Freud's discovery of the unconscious mind and with that acceptance relinquish his explicit or implicit claim to moral ascendancy over his clientèle. To those who cannot bring themselves to resolve this dilemma, Jung's psychology must be a Godsend.

INDEX

To facilitate reference the letters (F) and (J) have been inserted where the same or a similar term is used in a different sense by Freudian and Jungian psychologists respectively.

196

206

Edward Glover

Edward Glover is a leader in Freudian psychoanalysis in England. The author of many psychological works in addition to *Freud or Jung?*, he is noted for the witty **style** and the erudition of his writing.